QUADERNS D'ARQUITECTURA I URBANISME
n. 272 — Summer 2020

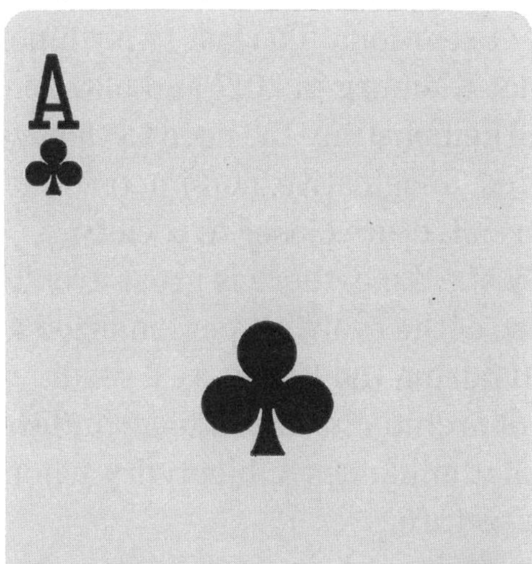

Biannual magazine of the COL·LEGI D'ARQUITECTES DE CATALUNYA (COAC)
Issue directed by FERRAN GRAU & NURIA CASAIS

Towards the end of the 1980s, Europe was moving towards a broader Union that was to culminate in the signing of the Maastricht Treaty in 1992. As a result of this community project, architects could be called from the public sphere to develop architectural and urban projects that invited a rethinking of a renewed identity. This moment was reflected in complex and optimistic projects such as the Zeebrugge Sea Terminal (1989) and the new National French Library (1989), both competition entries by the OMA studio. At the same time, in Switzerland, the studio formed by Jacques Herzog and Pierre de Meuron was gradually consolidating the construction of its own architectural language that pursued a "maximum ontological state of matter",[1] in which the surface and architectural composition were of particular importance. In relation to Herzog & de Meuron's work, Jeffrey Kipnis pointed out the attractive, seductive use of "cosmetic techniques"[2] that serve to activate subjectivity in the architectural experience.

After almost thirty years and various socioeconomic situations with moments of prosperity and recession, the European Union is undergoing a political and economic decline that is shaking its identity. The circumstances of each moment have influenced the way in which architecture is conceived and, consequently, the definition of architecture's appearance. Reacting to the different conditions, European architecture has built a diverse identity and currently faces a reality that calls for urgent responses and efficient solutions. The last two winners of the Mies van der Rohe Award (DeFlat Kleiburg in 2017 and 530 apartments—Grand Parc Bordeaux in 2019) demonstrate the need to value what already exists and highlight committed, imaginative, non-impositional strategies that are capable of bringing architecture closer to society.

Generally speaking, there is great architectural diversity in Europe, partly because of the evolving, personalized application of cosmetic techniques forged during the 1990s. As a result, we see full confidence in the possibilities of architectural language and the deployment of a cosmetic refinement that enhances subjectivity when it comes to designing and reading architecture.

As for the desire to bring architecture into the social sphere by using, among other strategies, an intentionally close, stripped back and unfinished language, it is worth mentioning cosmetic techniques like the one that seeks to recover, reinterpret and integrate rigorously the tradition and the very best of the modern movement, evoking past scenes (interiors and exteriors) that incorporate now-revised ornaments. Others, meanwhile, propose a domestic monumentality in which architecture becomes noble, kind and, at the same time, radical. Other cosmetic techniques define a modern, technical palimpsest in the search for languages that aim to integrate absolutely contemporary parameters. There is also increasing space for architecture that combines digital technologies and sustainable materials, in keeping with closed ecological cycles, and other important techniques in the European context that are used to build an architecture based on fragments, brutalism, and even cuts in the style of Matta-Clark.

The etymology of the term cosmetic combines the idea of order with that of ornament (beauty and image), creating a dual synergistic bond. In this sense, when Kipnis points out the creative capacity of the ornament-minimalism duality (understanding the latter as a kind of order), he highlights a certain contradiction in the cosmetic techniques of Herzog & de Meuron. It is precisely this apparently contradictory connection that gives rise to other very personal and extended cosmetic techniques, such as a contemporary version of the architecture of resistance[3] that seeks to perpetuate itself and resist the momentum of (planned) obsolescence of the language. This attitude of resistance sets out to achieve a timeless architectural status, where the author aims to go unnoticed by adopting an attitude that the British refer to as authorless. To this end, architecture uses a cosmetic technique comparable to the principles of nude,[4] with the predominance of "skin tones" characteristic of a consolidated historical context that aim to construct a kind of discreet camouflage.

With the extensive use of cosmetic techniques, ornament becomes a tool that takes on new meanings, wider-ranging and even less apparent. The unfinished, the discreet, the lavish or the technified, is also, then, in its own way, ornamented. Architecture is defined by artifice, often in layers, thicker (now the thickness is back) or thinner, revealing the cosmetic nature of the construction and the possibilities of a language taken to the extreme, and defining, up to this moment, the new on the basis of the syntactic domain of the old.

On this basis, *Quaderns* 272 sets out to analyse different cosmetic techniques by means of a critical approach organized on three levels, corresponding to three scales of the project. First, it looks at the current state of the face of the European city, constructed, reconstructed and transformed. Second, it debates the definition of the architectural object, analysing surface and depth, and, consequently, the idea of artifice from an external view of architecture as well as from a vision of the architecture of the public interior. Finally, like a digital zoom, cosmetic techniques are analysed by means of the study of the architectural fragment while simultaneously attending to the identity of the whole (The piece and the entirety). It is, precisely, the conception of this fragment, increasingly complex and relevant, that contains some of the keys to responding to a possible turn in the discipline of architecture. A turn that may not be so cosmetic.

Ferran Grau & Nuria Casais

1
ZAERA, Alejandro: "Continuities", interview with Herzog & de Meuron, *El Croquis*, No. 60, 1993.

2
KIPNIS, Jeffrey: "The Cunning of Cosmetics", *El Croquis*, No. 84, 1997.

3
CHIPPERFIELD, David: *Sergison & Bates 2G*, No. 34, Gustavo Gili, Barcelona, 2002.

4
Nude is a cosmetic technique that consists in applying make-up without appearing to, in order to achieve a natural, neutral appearance.

The Face of the City
Scale 1

The evolution of European cities continues to swing between the essence of the emotional city,[1] and the disorder and potential of new "urbanal" scenarios.[2] Historical, newly constructed and other radically transformed scenarios coexist within the same city. They all try to fit into an urban whole that tends to be redefined according to fragments, discontinuities and a changing idea of urbanity. The reaffirmation of a personal identity contrasts with the tendency towards globalization.

This first section brings together and analyses ten urban scenes belonging to five European cities (London, Paris, Milan, Copenhagen and Zurich). The search for a collective, reflective and conclusive reading describes what is seen and what is hidden, and above all takes stock of the successful or failed reconciliation of the *ville* and the *cité*.[3] The first is understood as the physically constructed environment, and the second is abstract in nature, like the character of urban life. This collective exercise based on the confrontation of scenes, then, aims to decipher the contemporary settings in which we live and to glimpse their future. When we look at the face of the city, we can make out different cosmetic techniques which, when brought together, define today's urban scenarios. It is then possible to assess their potential and their limitations in each specific context. The contrast of the ten urban scenes debates the ability of architecture collectively or individually to build the identity of a city, the sense of "homeyness",[4] memory, nostalgia, heterogeneity, and the hits and misses of contexts designed to live in.

1
CARUSO, Adam: "The Emotional City", *Quaderns d'Arquitectura i Urbanisme*, 2001.

2
MUÑOZ, Francesc: "Urbanalización: cuatro nuevos requerimientos urbanos", *Urbanalización. Paisajes comunes, lugares globales*, Gustavo Gili, Barcelona, 2008. "The urbanal city is a city with 'urbanal' places that explain the urban consequences of globalization."

3
SENNETT, Richard: *Building and Dwelling: Ethics for the City*, Allen Lane, London, 2018.

4
CARUSO, Adam, *op. cit.*: "Being in the city feels a certain way. This is similar to being at home, you know when you feel at home, when you can take off your shoes and relax. [...] The architectural vanguard has not recently much discussed the significance, or the defining characteristics of homeyness."

Guillermo López
London

Enric Llorach
Paris

Matilde Cassani
Milan

Nuria Casais & Ferran Grau
Copenhagen

André Bideau
Zurich

London

I

“It was a small mistake, but with great consequences. On September 2, 1666, Thomas Farrinor, baker to King Charles II of England, failed, in effect, to turn off his oven.”

Sometimes cities suffer wounds, on their skin or in their deeper structures, that transform their image forever. At one o’clock in the morning of that September 2, 1666, London began to be devastated by the Great Fire.

The diaries of Samuel Pepys have recorded the memory of that precise moment, revealing how a domestic anecdote could accelerate the transformation of the physiognomy and the image of an entire city. London’s architecture, with its narrow façades and timber-frame structures, was gradually replaced by an architecture made of brick and, specifically, by a new typology, the terraced house, which would, from then on, embody the archetypal essence of the city.

It seems interesting to analyse those sudden transformations, since any form of urban reconstructive surgery embodies a threefold debate which deals with preservation as a political form, with an ideological construction of the urban image, and with the speculative financial opportunities derived from it, which in many cases end up having a decisive influence on the previous ones.

That was exactly what happened in London after the fire, when a process of speculative urban development was initiated by, among others, Nicholas Barbon. Physicist and economist, as well as a savage entrepreneur, Barbon began to develop housing developments which included a whole row or a whole square—as in the case of Red Lion Square in Holborn—in order to economize and standardize building processes, giving way to a new form of uniformity that could begin to be observed in the streets and in the increasing number of piazzas that Inigo Jones had popularized a few decades before. A uniformity where only subtle differences in the façades, here and there, were able to introduce a minimum variability.

After the success of the method proposed by Barbon, the city could be understood as a form of modular repetition whose image restored, with only slight changes, a solid and orderly urban vision.

Perhaps that short financial episode of the city contains one of the most intimate connections between order (*kósmos* in Greek) and image, that combines the inner structure with the cosmetic surface, in which *kósmos* and *kosmetikós* go hand in hand. And, in passing, a good excuse to reflect on the urban assumptions of many of London’s contemporary financial urban processes.

II

Interiors are one of the most fragile parts of architecture. Perhaps because of their difficult preservation and their ever-changing image, they have often been excluded from the canonical histories of architecture and urbanism, though they sometimes contain clues as to the evolution and physiognomy of the city. One of those stories about interiors collected by architectural historiography has its origin 250 km north of London, in Chatsworth.

In a similar way to what happened at the beginning of the seventeenth century in the Netherlands, where tulips became powerful symbols of the wealth and power of certain families, success in the cultivation of strange exotic plants was a cause for entertainment and competition among the idle and dilettante Victorian aristocracy.

As Reyner Banham records in *The Architecture of the Well-Tempered Environment*, it was precisely Joseph Paxton who, shortly before working on the Crystal Palace, first achieved one of these botanical feats. He succeeded in growing a delicate giant water lily from Amazonia—the *Victoria Regia*—on British territory. In fact his success was due to the creation of a complex greenhouse equipped with an effective thermal regulation system that literally transformed architecture into an artificial climatic and atmospheric device.

Only five years earlier, Richard Burton had built the Palm House at Kew Gardens in London that illustrates this text. In this little fiction of a

tropical interior, it is not difficult to see the birth of a self-sufficient and generic architecture that quickly led to an unlimited and paradoxical repetition—as paradoxical as the innumerable, generically identical, autonomous and indifferent structures that populate sometimes antagonistic climatic, cultural or social contexts.

Undoubtedly, Paxton's invention marked the start of a cosmopolitan era in which incipient technological globalization developed tools (fateful, in hindsight) that served to relativize the idea of context by means of mechanisms such as the creation and use of artificial climates. The self-sufficiency of the interior was connected to the urban scale and, in its seemingly secondary role, it started to modify irreversibly the image of cities from within.

Paris

I

Boulogne-Billancourt, Paris. An excrescence from the Boulevard Périphérique, like an amputated stump. Above it, the Bois de Boulogne. Via the old Porte de Saint-Cloud enters one of Haussmann's axes, Avenue Pierre Grenier. Forming obtuse angles, two more lines, Avenue Edouard Vaillant and Route de la Reine.

Where Edouard Vaillant becomes Avenue du Général Leclerc, six more roads radiate from the Place Marcel. Above the Route de la Reine is the Prince-Marmottan district, in a right angle formed by the Parc des Princes to the east and Roland Garros to the north. At the intersection are the

Jardin de Serres and Porte d'Auteuil. Above Avenue de la Porte d'Auteuil is the Bois de Boulogne and, a little further to the west, the Parc de Boulogne-Edmond de Rothschild, Longchamp race course and the river Seine.

The École, Gymnase et Jardin Public Maître Jacques[1] is located in between the Route de la Reine, Villa Marie Justine, Rue de Paris and Rue Maître Jacques. The school comprises ten classrooms, an underground gymnasium, a school dining room, a leisure centre, four dwellings, parking and a public park. The site draws the entire city block together, as it is in contact with three streets. To the south, with a passage that connects with the Route de la Reine. To the east—towards Rue Maître Jacques—, is a public garden and a square. A volume of architecture is laid out along the street to the north, alongside Villa Marie Justine. The dwellings are grouped in three volumes and are attached to the school on its northern flank. In this way, the classrooms are drawn back from Villa Marie Justine and receive sunlight on the south side. Beneath this axis are the underground gym and the volume of the refectory.

The Maître Jacques public facility—which received the Prix grand public des architectures contemporaines de la Métropole Parisienne—stands out for an organization of public space that improves pedestrian connections on the one hand, and also serves to blur the borders between the public garden, the passage, the schoolyard and the gym. Even if—due to use requirements—, different spaces have an actual separation, perception encourages an idea of openness and a more plural and integrated public life. Accordingly, the longitudinal volume of the school opens up to the public space by means of a large porch-covered ground floor. The facility

1
École, Gymnase et Jardin Public Maître Jacques, Ateliers 234 architectes, 2005–2009. Site surface: 5,700 m², built area: 6,751 m², public space area: 3,300 m².

as a whole helps to patch up a piece of urban tissue which is often disintegrated in Prince-Marmottan, establishing its urban character as well as encouraging open-air activities in the sunlight and with shade.

II

In a meander of the Seine there is an elongated island, the Île Seguin. Next to it is the Île de Saint-Germain, larger but belonging to Issy-les-Moulinaux. In the southern-most part of the meander that constitutes Boulogne-Billancourt is Billancourt-Rives de Seine, where the Place Jules Guesde reproduces the distinctive Parisian node and its triangulated street lines. Between Rue Ives Kermen and the river is the site for the former Renault factory.[2] On the other bank—the convex side of the meander—, is Meudon, reaching the river via a slight slope caused by the erosion of the river bed. Billancourt-Rives de Seine stands on layers of sedimentation that produce an almost flat topography.

The Trapèze[3] comprises 32 ha including 515,000 m^2 dedicated to housing, offices and facilities, 17 ha of public space, seven of them public park. The master plan foresees a kind of block fractioned into large and irregular pieces.[4] The built volume is often modelled to emphasize both the contextual approach and its singularity.[5] Apart from the work on the volume, the Trapèze highlights the work on the facings, either because they involve rehabilitation,[6] or because they seek to define the singularity mentioned above. This use of cosmetic approaches ranges from mirroring façades[7] to postmodern porches.[8]

2
Starting out as a humble workshop opened in Boulogne-Billancourt back in 1898, Renault occupied during the 70s more than 100 ha at Boulogne-Billancourt, Île Seguin and Meudon (Hauts de Seine). Nationalized after WW2, privatized during the 90s, Renault is today delocalized and is associated with the Japanese giants Nissan and Mitsubishi. In 2017, Renault-Nissan-Mitsubishi was the leading automobile group in the world. The immense *forteresse ouvrière* closed its doors in 1992. Between 2004 and 2005, the Renault factory was demolished.

3
In 2000, SAEM Val de Seine Aménagement commissioned the sustainable master plan design Aménagement du Trapèze Renault / Rives de Seine to AAUPC (Chavannes & Associés). Taking part in the Trapèze were architecture studios from France and the rest of Europe like Diener & Diener Architekten, Josep Lluís Mateo, Jean Nouvel, Sauerbruch Hutton, Mikon Studio, PPA architects & Xavier Leplaë, Eliet & Lehmann architects, Brenac & Gonzalez & Associés, Beckmann-N'thepe architects, Studioninedots + Atelier 115, AZC, Antonini Darmon, Hamonic + Masson & Associés, Dominique Perrault, Chartier Dalix, Baumschlager Eberle, Agence Bernard Bühler, PHD architects, Xaveer de Geyter, Mecanoo, Patrick Chavannes, and Hondelatte Laporte architects. At the same time, Jean Nouvel designed the master plan for Île Seguin that was executed by the Japanese firm Shigeru Ban.

A 550

Desde JUNG tenemos el placer de presentaros nuestra nueva serie A 550, una magnífica reinterpretación de la serie A Creation, que aportará dinamismo y modernidad a cualquier estancia.

Disponibles en varias tonalidades, entre las cuales destacan el blanco y el negro mate, los mecanismos de la serie A 550, tras su montaje, quedan totalmente enrasados en la pared, una pincelada estética con la que no contaba su precursora.

In the central part of the image is the rehabilitation of the Boulogne Pont de Sèvres project and the Pont de Sèvres - Citylights towers. To the right is the Tour Horizons, the collage of architectures in the form of a ziggurat by Jean Nouvel. In the foreground, the Crèche de la Giraffe, from which the head of a giraffe emerges. This image shows one of the most distinctive traits of the Quartier du Forum: the staggering of architecture in its longitudinal section. [9]

From the pedestrian bridge to the right we see five people. A woman is walking down the last few metres of the bridge, and three men are walking on the concrete pavement. A boy crouched under a tree hugs his knees in a distracted manner. The pedestrians' movement alternates as they walk in opposite directions in a successive sequence. The scene is strange. This form of estrangement—which embodies a more aerial melancholy, closer to the data cloud and the world of images than to the flâneur walking among masses of people—finds an analogy with trees from the Quartier du Forum, available at any height, like in a Magritte painting. A kind of estrangement highlighted by the Crèche de la Giraffe, where the giraffe and the bear—big and monochrome—are intertwined with a staggered type of architecture. The giraffe, with its elongated neck, tries to reach leaves on one of the aerial trees.

Milan

I

Not so long ago, the site of Fondazione Feltrinelli was occupied by a famous Milanese plant nursery, Fratelli Ingegnoli. At first, it was shocking to think that this little corner of nature remaining in the centre of the city should be demolished to make way for a new building. At that time, the city of Milan and its residents were not used to major developments, though they were perhaps ready for this event.

Time has passed and, now, every time you walk past Fondazione Feltrinelli, you feel that Herzog & de Meuron designed a very traditional and expressively Milanese part of the city, as they termed it as the time.

The building is a bold, repetitive gesture, but the sensation it gives is one of a very delicate, well ordered intervention.

Nostalgically speaking, you might still miss the sensation of an impressive garden emerging from the old Spanish walls of the city, like in the days when the plant nursery was still open for business.

Urbanistically speaking, Fondazione Feltrinelli decidedly reconstructs a gateway identity, dialoguing directly with the old bastions of the walled

4
The Tours du Pont de Sèvres - Citylights rehabilitation project, by Dominique Perrault, comprises 919,230 m². The Boulogne Pont de Sèvres rehabilitated housing project, by Eliet & Lehmann architects, 50,000 m². A small project like the Crèche de la Giraffe, the school by Hondelatte Laporte, 1,450 m².

5
Examples are the work on the volume of the Ardeko buildings, by Baumschlager Eberle, and Office Boulogne-Billancourt, by Studioninedots + Ateliers 115.

6
As explained in note 4, Trapèze's emblematic projects Tours du Pont de Sèvres - Citylights and Boulogne Pont de Sèvres are rehabilitations.

7
See the use of mirroring façades in the projects Cap City Rives de Seine, by PPA architectures & Xavier Leplaë architect, Quai Ouest, by Brenac & Gonzalez & Associés, and the Office Building on Avenue Leclerc, by AZC. On façade dissolution see also the work by Stephane Malka at 3BOX92 using black monochrome.

8
See the interpretation of the Palazzo della Civiltà Italiana by Antonini Darmon at Boulogne Arches.

9
The staggering of the longitudinal section can be noticed in Boulogne-Pont de Sèvres and the Tour Horizons, but also in former projects like Residence Aquitaine. As well as other recent projects like the Primary School for the Sciences and Biodiversity, by Chartier Dalix architectes, or the 54 housing ZAC Seguin Rives de Seine, by PHD architectes.

town (Porta Volta), though the project has only been carried out partially.[1] To date, only one building has been completed, to one side of the gateway. The other, shorter building, pending construction, will stand on the other side of the street and be identical in its design. This second volume is expected to be built in the near future and is pending municipal approval for work to start.[2] The development was intended to be combined with a new linear park along the other side of the building. Although on one side, then, the linearity of the building reconstructs a frontage with a permeability that Ingegnoli did not have, the city still misses the splendid garden at the rear.

Milan could be called a private city, a city with limited green areas and public spaces, where the green areas mostly belong to incredible though walled gardens and courtyards. While the building's identity stands, pending completion by its symmetrical other side, the city does not yet have a new public park for its residents.

II

When Fondazione Prada opened its doors to the public in 2005, it was like discovering a new part of the city. The arts centre, situated on an industrial estate that was once home to a distillery, is a small city in itself. To quote Rem Koolhaas,[3] it comprises a series of buildings belonging to very different typologies. It is neither a remodelling project nor a new development; it stands as a stratified reality made up of the complexity of a district of the city. Old and new, high and low, narrow and wide coexist in a series of buildings that could be experienced as a sequence of interior spaces to be discovered, one by one, though the overall image of the place is that of a single identity. The building that completes the sequence is a tower rising up from an incredibly vast landscape left empty by an old railway station.

But where is Fondazione Prada? Before, this area was a rather disconnected part of the city, from infrastructures and urban activities alike. In this sense, the series of units that make up the arts centre seem like a smaller part of a rediscovered, renovated neighbourhood in the city, ready to expand into its surroundings.

This site actually belongs to a larger railway system that recently became the focus of Milan's urban expansion, reconnecting centre and periphery. Its future was reimagined in a series of international competitions and public commissions. Lately, Scalo Romana was designated as the site of the future Olympic Village of Milan 2026.

The Fondazione Prada tower can, then, be likened to Patrick Geddes' Outlook Tower, a kind of observatory of the city's social and physical phenomena, fundamental aspects of urban planning based on an evolving theory of human settlements. Once again, Milan chooses a big event to promote its identity to an international public, as it did with Expo 2015, while the tower dominates the city and awaits the results of an attempted future development, yet to be discovered.

1
The plan designed by Herzog & de Meuron proposed two buildings, one on each side of the existing bastions, reinforcing the idea of a gateway.

2
The first side was developed by a private venture, in agreement with the Comune di Milano. The second side is strictly public, as is the park. Herzog & de Meuron designed the entire development, including the garden.

3
Article published at https://www.domusweb.it/it/architettura/2015/05/11/fondazione_prada_a_milano.html

I

Nordhavn, the northern port, gives its name to the largest metropolitan development in Scandinavia. Construction on it began at the end of the nineteenth century, and it is located four km from the centre of Copenhagen with exceptional connections by land and sea. Nordhavn extends over the Øresund Strait on land reclaimed from the sea[1] to house a constructed area of 4,000,000 m^2, where 40,000 inhabitants will live and 40,000 jobs be created. With the aim of being a sustainable city of the future,[2] the urban project (COBE, 2008) integrates debate between citizens and developers. The district of Aarhusgade, the first to be developed in Nordhavn, seeks consolidation, continuing the district of Østerbro, despite the infrastructure barriers that separate them. Aarhusgade is the result of the transformation of an industrial sector into an urban residential space, with production and an economy typical of the tertiary sector.[3]

Strolling through Göteborg Square we leave behind a stepped waterfront, a sign of a new urbanity, and looking towards the north, we see an urban space that includes three of the most representative buildings of the old and the new Nordhavn: Portland Towers (DesignGroup), The Silo (COBE) and Frihavns Tårnet (Praksis).[4] Different cosmetic techniques define a new architectural identity in which only Portland Towers display the existence of an industrial port structure, covered with a volume of can-

1
According to the data provided by By & Havn, the area reclaimed from the sea in Nordhavn accounts for 1 % of the total area of Copenhagen. The filler material used for the new growth comes from the island of Zealand itself, and approximately 16 % comes from the excavation of the Copenhagen Circular Metro line.

2
CPH City & Port Development participates in the EnergyLab Nordhavn strategic partnership, which focuses on the development of intelligent energy systems, providing the energy flexibility necessary for the efficient use of renewable energy. A sustainable urban development process is the backbone of a sustainable city with a high degree of habitability. For this reason, the new areas of the city in Nordhavn are certified according to DGNB sustainability standards. Sustainability in Nordhavn can be experienced and measured.

3
The new container and cruise port moves to a new extension of the same port (northeast), occupying new land reclaimed from the sea (Ydre Nordhavn).

4
The Portland towers are the result of the transformation of two concrete silos built by Aalborg Portland in 1979; The Silo and the Frihavns Tårnet are the result of the adaptation of two silos built by the DLG company.

tilevered offices fortified with industrial-style bracing, and finished with an enveloping curtain wall. In Nordhavn, what you don't see is important: in the Frihavns Tårnet building, for example, electricity, light and heat are controlled by automatic sensors that measure CO_2 levels and temperature. This means the temperature and the indoor climate are regulated automatically. On the other hand, what is evident (and visible) in Nordhavn is part of a new style that gives it an identity of its own.

In the centre of the image, a high-rise car park (Lüders, JAJA arkitekten) houses a recreational public space on its roof covering an area of 2,400 m². At a height of 24 m, and after climbing 135 steps lined with planters and the history of Nordhavn printed on the metal façade, we recover the view of the sea and the centre of Copenhagen. In the foreground of the image, a cyclist in motion makes a move to position and orient himself as he moves forward in the middle of a dynamic and constantly growing urban context.

II

The final section of the M1 Metro line traces a dramatic straight line. Raised above ground level, it establishes the urban and territorial identity of the district of Ørestad, located ten minutes from the centre of Copenhagen. The M1 line circulates on an intermittent concrete bridge just after the Sundby station in the direction of Vestamager, the final stop; in this way, the M1 ensures urban connection and the crossing paths of other infrastructures across the city.

Ørestad is an artificial city developed in a wetland area in the south of the island of Amager, and construction began thanks to the sale of publicly owned land to private interests.[5] Ørestad was conceived in the late 1980s as a strategy to alleviate the main problems of the city of Copenhagen: low growth, unemployment and debt. Near the two important infrastructures of the airport and Øresund bridge, which links Copenhagen and Malmö, it offset the tendency of the capital to grow towards the north.

The initial plan included mainly housing and offices, and currently includes educational facilities, a large shopping centre (Field's), an international convention centre (Bella Center)[6] and a multipurpose venue (Royal Arena) with global ambitions.

Ørestad is, in itself, a new major axis that divides an urban fabric woven of single-family homes with gardens, a golf course and wetlands. The duality of large and small scale coexists in Ørestad, where the architectural organization resulting from the building sites and interests of private development combines terraced houses with allotments and large housing blocks.

5
Together with Ørestad, it was decided to build the subway which would significantly improve public transport in the capital.

6
In Ørestad, signs have been installed to announce the identity of this district, and they provide different messages:

"With roots in Copenhagen architecture and lifestyle, Bellakvarter shows how a local neighbourhood can coexist beautifully with an international conference centre."

"A new Copenhagen neighbourhood is in the making right here! The area around Bella Center is transforming into Bellakvarter—with residents, shops and visitors from all over the world."

"Just around the corner, you will find Nordergarden—a new urban space that during the coming summers will become a hotspot for urban gardens, play, good food and events for all of Copenhagen. In the middle of Nordgarden the Bella Urban Garden community is growing. Here you will find radishes, apple trees, flowers and everything in between. During the summer, there are free workshops on urban gardening."

In Ørestad, water is another structural element involved in a personal way of understanding the urban landscape that connects with the nature of the place. A canal parallels the route of the M1, and a pond defines the southern limit of this promised land that looks out towards the natural area of Vestamager, also known as Kalvebod Fælled.[7] On the southern edge, the architecture of Ørestad is abruptly interrupted by the presence of the horizon. 8 House (BIG), on the southern limit of Ørestad, reveres the landscape by tilting its architecture and inviting nature to be part of its dynamic courtyards, defined by small mountains—real ones, this time.

Zurich

I

As much as Lake Zurich and the rivers Limmat and Sihl define the urban territory, Zurich's morphology is marked by the broad stream of tracks that leave the centre in a north-westerly direction. As a sequence of rail yards with numerous lines branching off, this historic separation splits large parts of the city into two halves, offering only a few connections such as the Hardbrücke viaduct. Georg Aerni's image cuts across this characteristic infrastructural void leading into Zurich Hauptbahnhof station.

Traditional buildings of the nineteenth-century neighbourhood frame its central perspective through an everyday street. In its centre the view presents an open space beyond which rises a vast new development. This monolithic backdrop is separated from the foreground by an old petrol

7
Area reclaimed from the sea in the 1940s to house military manoeuvres, and which is currently structured as a natural marshland space.

station and a humble house, which both abut the train tracks. The left foreground of the image is dominated by the massive historical building of Zürcher Brockenhaus, the traditional thrift store. It is indicative of the working class identity of this part of Zurich, now in transition. Dealing with used clothing, furniture and household items, Brockenhaus belies an earlier economic logic of reuse. Yet the image also presents a stage prepared for an entirely new scale of urban development.

Though increasingly busy with train traffic, the fringes of the main rail yard have recently succumbed to intense development pressure. After decades of unsuccessful planning to cover the tracks with a platform, a vast urbanization project for both rail yard edges was initiated in the 2000s. The Europaallee business district, the first phase of this project, was nearing completion when the photo was taken. Its centre shows scaffolding that indicated an upcoming rail yard development project, which since has been initiated on this side of the tracks. The neorealist scenery is therefore history, as is the view across the rail yard. The site is both an example of the substantial densification process that Zurich is currently undergoing, as it also demonstrates the change in strategy of the Swiss national railway, following an internal reorganization that made the latter a private property developer and investor on its own land.

The quotidian nature of Aerni's urban scene only hints at an upheaval which is the result of decisions on the national level that were made less than twenty years ago. Typically, cycle trafffic on urban land is a dynamic that characterizes the periphery and its sites of former industrial production. But in the case of redeveloped rail yards this periphery no longer represents an edge condition; it is now a newfound centrality.

The contemporary architecture visible as a backdrop in Aerni's photo is indicative of the Europaallee master plan which has been implemented in several phases since approval by the citizens of Zurich in 2006. In order to garner voter support for the influx of private capital on such an unprecedented scale, the master plan broke down the project into a sequence of similar parcels with a unifying morphological agenda. As proposed by Kees Christiaanse, footprints pick up the grain of the nineteenth-century morphology and extend the geometry of certain streets into the former rail yard service zone. Above this dense footprint, each field morphs into a sequence of towers, usually sprouting two or three volumes. Although squat in comparison to recent developments in Zurich West, the sequence of towers at Europaallee creates a distinct skyline. These signature boxes—office towers and luxury rentals—denote the new business centre as one enters the main station. Moreover, the density of the continuous plinth produces a picture-perfect urban spectacle at ground level, alive with sponsored culture, hipster retail and upscale dining. Tellingly, the main tenant is no longer the Swiss banking behemoth UBS, but Google, operating its largest campus in Europe at Europaallee.

Obviously such implants are seen as fragments of maximum return, clad in sophisticated architecture—designed by the usual suspects such as Caruso St. John, Wiel Arets, Max Dudler, Gigon Guyer or David Chipperfeld. Regardless of contextualist overtures, the massive strip of mixed-use development in turn impacts the adjacent neighbourhood—an area already undergoing its own process of gentrification. On either side of the rail yard public opinion has traditionally been characterized by activism and resistance to urban overdevelopment, with May 1 demonstrations producing violent acts against ground floor cafes in the early years of Europaallee.

Nevertheless a final judgement on the downtown extravanganza has yet to be made. Undoubtedly, Europaallee is a testimony to a learning curve in Zurich. To some extent, Christiaanse's master plan has produced heterogeneity of program and tangible urban form. These achievements must be taken into account after decades of failed attempts to deliver property developments either above the rail yard or along the Sihl river adjacent to the station—itself the object of brutal redevelopment schemes during the 1960s. Europaallee is therefore also a testimony to the Swiss tradition of political accountability that often fells projects on such a large scale and has little tolerance for grand urban gestures.

II

The image is characterized by its great depth, achieved by the photographer's elevated position. Over a remnant of small-scale urban fabric and some greenery, the gaze is first drawn to the office tower by Gigon Guyer that occupies the middle ground of the image, then beyond to a misty horizon. Groups of high-rise towers appear in the distance, their succession emphasizing the strong perspective of the image.

Photographer Rasmus Norlander is poised atop a temporary structure: a miniature tower fabricated out of fifteen freight containers, stacked and made accessible to showcase Freitag bags.

Developed and initially manufactured in this neighbourhood, the bags are made out of the truck tarpaulins. Thus fashion repeats the recyling logic that has come to characterize the redevelopment of Zurich West from former industrial use to an office and residential zone.

The logic of real estate led to the disappearance of the creative industries after a transitional period, in the 1990s, when graphic designers, architects, artists, galleries and clubs flocked to vacant industrial sites in the area. Today they exist elsewhere except for small footprints in Zurich West, such as the mentioned Freitag Tower or the ZHDK school rising in the rear of the Norlander's image, a design by EM2N architects. The lavish conversion of a former dairy factory was one of the largest real-estate ventures by a private developer in Zurich. As a public-private partnership ZHDK includes not only schools for visual and performing arts and social work, but also market-rate apartments and a large parking garage.

We are looking at a case study of a postindustrial landscape where not only has physical production been halted and value redistributed, but where temporality has been altered. This also pertains to the interaction between buildings and the traffic infrastructure dominating Norlander's image: a Y-shaped expressway overpass with twin ramps that seems to weave the loose configuration of buildings together, defining an elevated platform over the existing streetscape. Shown uncharacteristically devoid of traffic, the vast empty plane gives the image a *pittura metafisica* quality.

A different modernity is invoked by the freeing up of urban ground for pedestrians which appears as an involuntary reference to CIAM's Athens Charter. Moreover, the almost intimate relationship between the viaduct and the architectural objects with their iconography of serialization appears as a covert reference to Ludwig Hilberseimer.

The viewpoint produces the illusion of a systemic relationship between buildings and raised traffic—the opposite is the case, as the redevelopment of Zurich West was fragmented and dictated by private interests, as in the case of ZHDK.

The road infrastructure has a fraught history itself. Hardbrücke, undergoing heavy use during most of the day, is the centerpiece of an inner city expressway linking outlying districts, and it has been repeatedly upgraded. Since the image was taken, it has been transformed to accommodate a tram line, and it is also a connector to Hardbrücke regional train station. Initially the viaduct was seen as a necessary temporary link for expressways still ending at the city limits. Since its inception in the 1970s, Hardbrücke has been criticized as a symbol of the invasive presence of motor traffic in the inner city, with opposition to the traffic planning leading to numerous demonstrations in Zurich. More recently, a domestication of the viaduct took place: not only was the tram line added in 2016, but also the proximity of clubs and high-end real-estate have somewhat shifted general perception, as the space under Hardbrücke became a spine along which different publics circulate in this changing neighbourhood.

This section brings together three projects located in three major European cities, which show three different ways of becoming integrated into the urban fabric. Clerkenwell 15 (London) is new-built, a small residential building with an office designed after an exhaustive study of the memory and the identity of the place. Its materialization illustrates the extreme possibilities of cosmetic techniques when it comes to defining an unexpected appearance and responding to a consolidated historical context. The social controversy associated with the construction of this building, resolved positively by legal means, is the most obvious testimony to the fierce debate about urban identity. The Chris Marker university residence (Paris) is a large building cut through by an imposing diagonal that reveals internal circulation and dominates the urban scale by dividing the building into two parts. The built volume becomes infrastructural, constructed over a depot and repair shop for eight bus routes of Paris public transport (RATP). The collective space laid out around the inner courtyard organizes the stepped rear façade, while the repetition of private space characterizes the main façade that looks onto the street. In an old industrial district, the Prada Foundation (Milan) reflects on contemporary materiality by means of an abstract approach. The relation between the old (apparently untouched or radically gilded) and the new is defined cosmetically in the lower volumes, where mirrored surfaces and an aluminium foam facing present a stony identity.

Groupwork + Amin Taha
15 CLERKENWELL CLOSE, London, 2017

Today Clerkenwell Close is mostly made up of mid-to-late twentieth century half-brick stretcher-bond pseudo-pastiche façades, making it impossible to tell quite which period or architectural language they represent. 15 Clerkenwell Close replaces one of these and aims in some way to better connect and represent the past with a broader contextual understanding than skin-deep imitation, at first contemporary but reminding us of the all but vanished eleventh-century limestone Norman abbey. Founded by Baron Jordan Briset for Augustinian nuns following the Conquest, it was expanded and remodelled until the sixteenth-century Protestant revolution brought about its dissolution. This precipitated a gradual erosion of the enclave which was at first appropriated as a single palace for the Duke of Newcastle, then subdivided into grand houses for the newly Protestant barons following the duke's son's beheading, then cleared again by a republican revolution to make way for Oliver Cromwell's London house.

Following Cromwell's death the restoration of the monarchy saw his house replaced with further subdivision into smaller rental properties, which, by London's nineteenth-century expansion and mass immigration, briefly housed Marx and a visiting Lenin. The last area of the abbey, its dining hall, was ignominiously used as a furniture showroom before a fire and the 1970s left only a few stones and the road layout as a memory. Whether Norman invasion, the killing of Wat Tyler and his Peasants' Revolt, Protestantism, republicanism, the printing presses that fuelled these and grew from leafleting into book and newspaper trades, later attracting Marx, Engels and Lenin to write for and use William Morris's Twentieth Century Press (now the Marx Library), Clerkenwell has had a history of radicalism outside the city gates with the changing of the times, and physically changing with them.

Building anew within this context has to raise more questions than how to fit in with the 1970s and '80s façade pastiches. Half brick-thick stretcher bonds and poor solid-to-void proportions already betray a lack of understanding of period proportions and details. That they hide poorly lit deep-plan office floor plates and cellular flats alike only adds to a disingenuous claim of respecting context and fitting in. Shouldn't we question whether architecture in the form of façade composition for such purposes is to be the future of our architectural heritage and, in turn, our broader cultural development? We'd be somewhat perplexed if music, the visual arts, or indeed the sciences limited their outlook and innovations to a criterion of fitting in. Perhaps, then, this is more a question of whether architects, after several generations of mastering two-dimensional façade play, have lost their literacy of the materials that first defined those compositions? The innate structural and textural properties, the poetic possibilities of their architectonic and symbolic composition? The Normans brought with them the use of limestone fresh from the quarry as it remained soft enough to carve and key together before calcifying to make stronger fortifications. Solid brick walls became the prevalent domestic and standard construction until the early twentieth century. The coming of steel and concrete frames, and arguably for better weathering, fire and structural integrity, allowed façade and structure to become ideas that could and would remain separate. Potentially leaving generations of architects without the knowledge, skills and, in turn, poetic possibilities of unifying both. Whether timber, stone, metal, glass, plastics or graphene, these have intrinsic structural, textural/tactile properties and, in the case of clip-on pseudo brick, though perhaps initially misjudged, potential for wit and humour as well as expediency. Understanding their nature allows us to use them literally or to subvert and play with them for symbolic meaning and wit.

In Clerkenwell, self-finished materials such as stone and brass, carved and fallen columns, revealed cloisters, pebble mosaic floors and scallop-shell handles at first express a reuse of load-bearing technologies to define architecture and allude to a local social/historical archaeology. With street level and tactile elements including scallop-shell door handles and Ionic capitals perhaps cryptically reminding us that the adjacent St James, like the Spanish Santiago de Compostela and all of us, has its footings in a predecessor. In Clerkenwell, the chapel of St Mary's within the vanished abbey; in Spain, in the Roman temple to Venus where the pagan pilgrims would leave scallop shells to symbolize her birth.

The building accommodates eight apartments, and two floors of open-plan and double-height office space sit within loose-fit column-free floor plates that allow future change of use and layouts by removing the internal oak utility furniture that defines their adjacent spaces. Previously unkempt land to the south has been landscaped to serve occupants and neighbours and be incorporated into the narrative of abbey remains with new pebble mosaics and further part-carved medieval stonework. A biodiverse roof provides two beehives, bird nests and habitat for invertebrates. Four mature trees are used to soak up 90% of the average annual rainfall and therefore avoid rainwater attenuation tanks and further basement excavation. A glazed solar chimney is placed on top of the stair and lift core with a rainproof open glazed overhang to allow natural smoke ventilation and therefore avoid mechanical equipment, an increased carbon footprint and running/maintenance costs. The use of stone as superstructure reduces the embodied carbon of the overall superstructure by 90% compared to steel or concrete frames. Reason enough to promote the reuse of stone for such purposes, though its dressing, in this instance quarry-found fossilized coral and ammonite shells, can give way to any taste in other designs.

Second floor

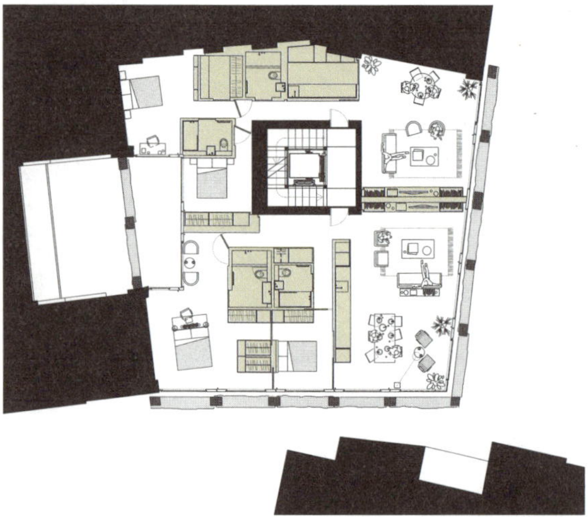

Ground floor

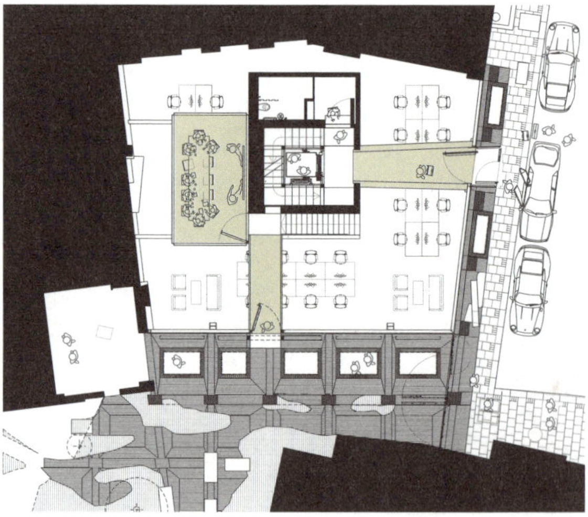

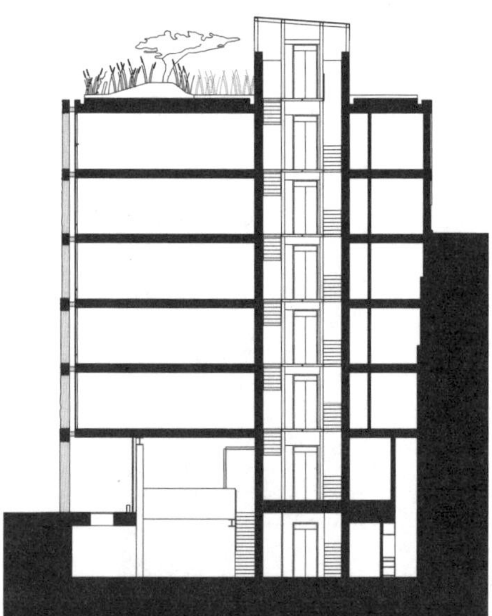

20
SJ10 AYY

Éric Lapierre Experience
CHRIS MARKER STUDENT HOUSING
AND RATP BUS FACILITIES, Paris, 2007–2018

The Chris Marker student residence defines a new standard for university housing by dramatically expanding collective spaces devoted to social interactions, thus transforming it into a kind of social condenser. Trusting in the power found in the formal organization of space, common areas are located on each level to improve the efficiency of this expansion: whatever level students live on, they have a common area close by.

These areas create a diagonal cascade of space running through the whole building from bottom to top to bring the urban energy of the boulevard below all the way to the last floor. This diagonal is carved out of the mass of individual apartments to improve the dialectical relationship between intimacy and collectivity and give the façade a specific identity. All these collective spaces (a series of double-height common areas arranged at each level—work rooms, cafeteria, etc.), are linked one to the other by an oblique elevator running along the main façade. Half (400 m^2) of the common areas are indoor lounges, and half are outside patios linked to the inside.

The whole building functions as a condensed city: gangways and corridors are its streets, apartments (365) its houses, indoor common areas public buildings, outside patios public squares, and the oblique lift its public transportation system. The whole building (100 m long and 31 m high) is built on a superimposed parking and repair garage that we have built for eight lines of Parisian public transport buses (RATP). In this way, industrial facilities are absorbed into the urban fabric and also serve as a pretext for the construction of public housing.

The Chris Marker residence is made of site-cast concrete. No holes for the forms and no expansion joints make the building fit naturally into the Parisian tradition of stone city.

The Chris Marker student residence is a reflection on domestic monumentality, the condition in which an apartment building passes a certain critical mass to engage, by its dimensions, in a monumental rapport with the public space. The apartments are served by external passages that turn into a corridor. Measuring 2.50 m wide, they are a twofold reflection on the need to define distinct functional areas to increase their perceived size, and to integrate the additional surface area made necessary by the application of accessibility standards for people with disabilities in living spaces, making bathrooms central spaces.

The residence reinterprets the typological imagination of the Modern Movement, some of the most beautiful examples of which are built on the other side of the street, in the Cité internationale universitaire (Swiss and Brazilian pavilions of Le Corbusier, Willem's house in the Netherlands, Marinus Dudok, etc.). But it is a product of the urban culture of Paris, thanks in particular to the stable tectonics given by site-cast concrete, while being fully glazed, like some seventeenth-century French mansions which are veritable stone grids with many perforations.

LE PLAISIR DU BIO
30

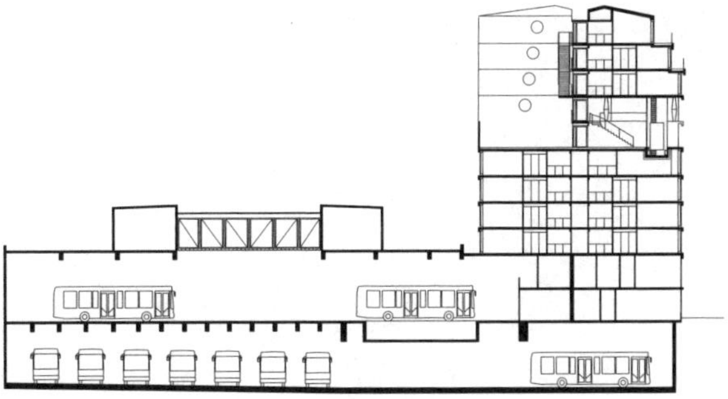

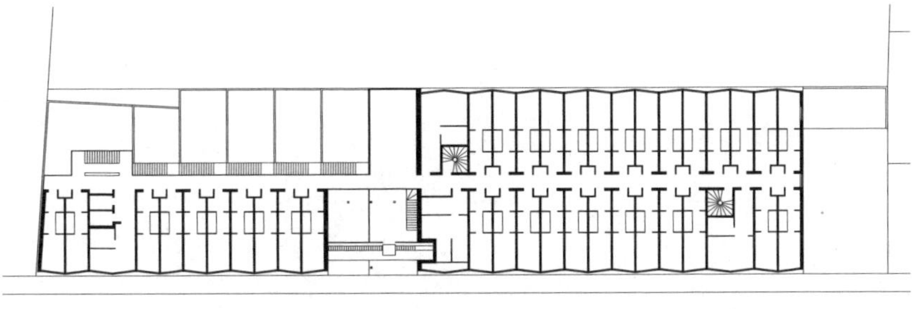

Seventh floor

Ground floor

LOXAM

EUROPONT
500 kg
67
FOIRE DE PARIS
27 OCT - 5 NOV

OMA
FONDAZIONE PRADA, Milan, 2008–2018

Located in a former gin distillery dating from 1910 in the Largo Isarco industrial complex on the southern edge of Milan, the new home of Fondazione Prada is a coexistence of new and regenerated buildings including warehouses, laboratories and brewing silos, as well as new buildings surrounding a large courtyard.

The complex aims to expand the repertoire of spatial typologies in which art can be exhibited. The project consists of seven existing buildings and three new structures: Podium, a space for temporary exhibitions; Cinema, a multimedia auditorium; and Torre, a nine-storey permanent exhibition space for displaying the foundation's collection and activities.

Within the perimeter of the Largo Isarco complex there were two freestanding structures: one flat and square, and the other more vertical. On close inspection, the square building did not offer attractive possibilities and was demolished, enabling the courtyard to become a significant element for open-air use.

The Deposito, an existing building on the west edge of the complex, is adapted for curatorial ingenuity: in its basement, the Fondazione's collection is arranged in a hybrid of strict storage and partial display, creating chambers where work such as a fleet of artists' cars can be unpacked or half-opened to the public.

The freestanding object to the east of the Great Hall, dubbed the Cisterna, is divided into three rooms with three interior pulpits connected to an exterior balcony. Its configuration suggests a precise industrial need that now reads as a quasi-religious environment.

The Cinema acts as an autonomous cell within the compound. With large bi-fold doors, it can be instantly connected to the courtyard. Inside, the raked seating can be converted into a flat floor, allowing the space to be used for staging outdoor events or as additional, covered gallery space.

Four houses that face the courtyard to the north and an abandoned garden to the south accommodate Fondazione offices and permanent galleries. Within their confines sits the Haunted House, an existing building with its exterior covered entirely in gold leaf. Inside, the intimate scale of its interiors generates a domestic setting for specific works.

Adjacent, the Podium forms the centre of the compound, sitting at the intersection of the two perpendicular axes through the site. This addition combines two volumes of very different qualities: a fully glazed, column-free podium on the ground floor. Resting on top is another gallery space clad in aluminum foam, with a bubbled pattern. Both galleries provide large multipurpose areas for temporary exhibitions and events.

Situated on the north-west corner of the compound, the Tower houses site-specific installations, as well as a restaurant, a reception space and guest facilities. The other floors, with gradually increasing heights, will accommodate site-specific installations and provide alternating views of the compound and the city.

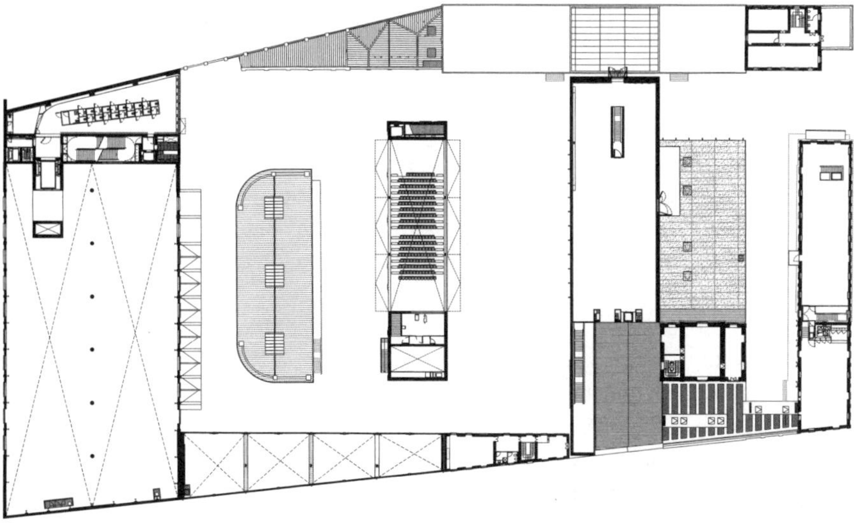

First floor

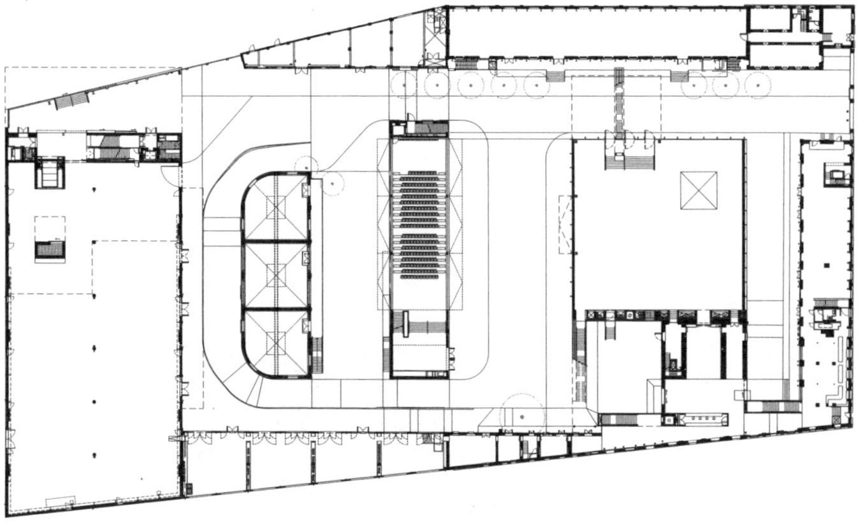

Ground floor

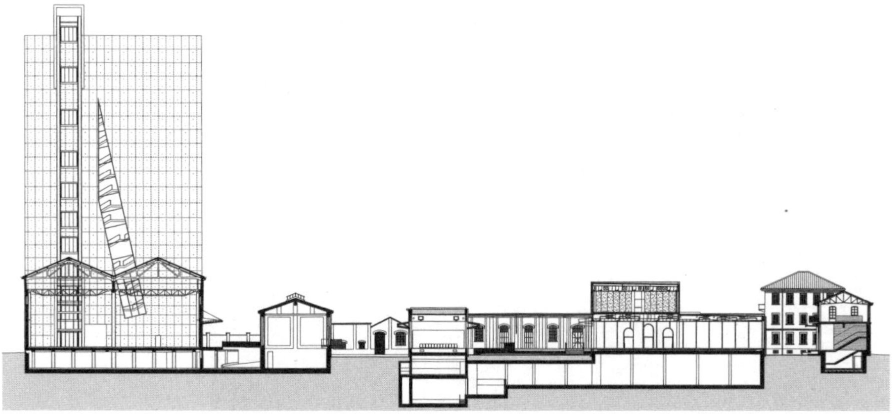

Repertoire

It is surprising that the enormous expansion of the art system has taken place in a reduced number of typologies for displaying art. To apparently everybody's satisfaction, the abandoned industrial space has become art's default preference—attractive because its predictable conditions do not challenge the artist's intentions—enlivened occasionally with exceptional architectural gestures.

The new Fondazione Prada is projected in a former industrial complex too, but one with an unusual diversity of spatial environments. To this repertoire, we are adding three new buildings—a large exhibition pavilion, a tower, and a cinema—so that the new Fondazione Prada represents a genuine collection of architectural spaces in addition to its holdings in art.

The Fondazione is not a preservation project and not new architecture. Two conditions that are usually kept separate here confront each other in a state of permanent interaction—offering an ensemble of fragments that will not congeal into a single image or allow any part to dominate the others.

New, old, horizontal, vertical, wide, narrow, white, black, open, enclosed—all these contrasts establish the range of oppositions that define the new Fondazione. By introducing so many spatial variables, the complexity of the architecture will promote unstable, open programming, where art and architecture will benefit from each other's challenges.

Rem Koolhaas

Surface and Depth
Scale 2

The architectural object is the habitual centre of attention in the debate about the management of cosmetic subjectivity and scientific objectivity, and today serves as a meeting point for the meanings of the face of the city and a constructive fragment of the whole. Surface and depth, exterior and interior, and what is seen and what is haptic and real come together in the architectural object. In this debate, it is important to remember that the order of the prevailing visual culture alters and conditions the design processes that make it possible, for example, for the virtual image to appear to be hyperreal—the return of the old debate that confronts poetry and rationality.[1]

Today, the artifice intrinsic in the architectural act continues to draw out meanings and interpretations that regulate the freedom of all those who experience architecture, and signal a constant revision of its democratic and social nature. Outer and inner appearances define the links with the city. Specifically from the outside, the architectural object chooses to be either contextual, autonomous or indifferent, and shows itself, then, to be friendly, distant, or unconcerned and alien to that which surrounds it. The architecture of the public interior, meanwhile, seen as an extension of the exterior, is also capable of managing its capacity and its potential when it comes to forming part of the city.

In a broader sense within the architectural discipline, the exterior-interior relationship paradoxically becomes increasingly hermetic in technical terms, raising the question as to whether it is possible, and necessary, to guarantee continuity between interior and exterior, as posited by the Modern Movement and many postmodern architectures.

1
The Lisbon Architecture Triennial held in 2019, entitled The Poetics of Reason, reaffirms the validity of the debate raised by the use of different cosmetic techniques in the field of the architectonic discipline. "The Poetics of Reason states that, for all its subjective and non-scientific dimension, architecture does rest on reason, and its aim is to shed light onto the specificity of this reason." Excerpt from the text published in the official brochure of the Lisbon Architecture Triennial (3 October to 2 December 2019).

Pep Avilés

Image (T)Acts

"Everything seems to indicate that we are facing a new cultural paradigm. In a short time we have gone from an architectural culture that was almost exclusively penned and technical to an eminently visual one."[1] This is possibly the strongest statement of the introduction to the new series of "authors" with which *Quaderns d'Arquitectura i Urbanisme* magazine began its most recent stage. Certainly, the visual skills of the new generation of architects, as well as the immediate availability of images that the internet industry provides, has facilitated this transition from the technical to the visual; or if you prefer, from the tectonic to the plastic. As Moisés Puente noted, this rapid passage in architecture culture questions novelty as a category, which is reconsidered this time—as happened in many other episodes of modernity—as a spectre of the past.

But there is something more significant in the transition to visual values in today's architectural culture that I would like to underscore: whether this emphasis on the image does not in turn entail a new order—that is, a new cosmetic. Let us briefly remember the etymological link between the words 'order' and 'ornament', both related to the word *kósmos*, which originally referred to ordering, arranging and preparing, but also to ornament. If this new order exists, we face new subjectivities mediated and propitiated by the photographic lens and other digital media that generate and facilitate a new form of representation. This subjectivity emerges at the intersection between the subject and the constellations of digital images with which this subject is surrounded. Are not these images the new trinkets of the present, signs of identity with which both architects and designers and their spaces and architectures are presented? Is not the technical and compositional capacity of architecture understood as an image, the way in which these spaces are currently organized?

Let us briefly recall an episode of modernity. It is known that the architect Pierre Koenig felt uncomfortable with the famous images that New York photographer Julius Shulman took of his Stahl house. The reason for his discomfort was the fact that these images—with the vast urban view of

Fig. 1

Fig. 2

Fig. 3

Los Angeles in the background—soon explained the house in its entirety and in a different way from what he intended even before he had completed it (fig. 1).[2] In fact, with his snapshots, the photographer had diverted the concept of the house: from the precise, industrial and serial production to which Koenig aspired, to the promotion of the modern bachelor lifestyle of cocktail parties that the photographer portrayed, the house ended up staging a completely different cultural reality. In few photographs taken hours before the night views, we see how Schulman faced an incomplete construction, where concrete finishes and other details had still to be done (fig. 2). With the help of vegetation, furniture and lighting, and thanks to the presence of his assistants—improvized models on the scene, conveniently dressed to convey the image of opulence characteristic of postwar American society—, Schulman constructed the night images that quickly became widespread, either in black and white including female models, or in colour including a male figure (fig. 3). Once these photographs circulated, Koening's technical and pragmatic concepts were eclipsed by the integrated materiality of Schulman's image constructions. This is just an example of how architecture has remained constructively unfinished until it acquires its photographic form, but also of the interrelatedness of built spaces and images, as well as the complex conceptual and spatial interplay that occurs between objects and subjects in the snapshots.

It is worth asking, then, what are the rules of a new *kósmoi* in the digital age and how are they materialized; if there is a new visual order through which a new generation of architects express themselves, one might ask how are these new subjectivites constructed? Is harmony between architecture and the media not one of the fundamental projects of modernity? Has there not been a constant and tireless attempt to merge subject and image during the past century, maximized by the complicity of the innumerable means of technical reproduction? Is there any possibility of establishing effective, shared subjectivities? The fundamental difference between images in our postmodern technical culture and the visual forms of the past is their dematerialization. Or, in other words, their radical homogeneity as binary digital code makes them suitable for circulation through mobile screens, computers, tablets, etc. Our interaction with them is digital in every way: technological and tactile. We interact with them through layers that record the electromagnetic mechanisms between the human body and the technological reproduction apparatus of the moment. The images circulate in the psychological space of the haptic, where image and touch are intimately related to express rejection or desire, approval, contempt, or indifference—that is, to mediate between our affections and our actions. I am interested in analysing this symbiosis, which that occurs between the tactile and the photographic as a form of

1
Puente, Moisés, "Local/Visitor", *Quaderns d'Arquitectura i Urbanisme*, No. 270, Barcelona, 2018, p. 9.

2
The architect and history professor at Liverpool University, Neil Jackson, recently published his industrial materialism, and the episode of the photographs taken by Julius Schulman. Jackson, Neil, *Pierre Koenig: A View from the Archive*, Getty Research Institute, Los Angeles, 2019.

new shared materiality and, therefore, as a contemporary cosmetic and organizational form. Hasn't the endless proliferation of textures, patterns and etchings on the architectural surfaces of the last fifteen years been a symptom of this fusion and the prelude to more complex forms of identification between subject and image? The assimilation of the image as an ornamental expression, as well as the definition of ornament as an image, achieves two objectives: on the one hand, it displaces ontologically what modernity understood as superficial, making the debate regarding the decorative more sophisticated; and, on the other, it reminds us of the architectural reliance of complex ornamental systems operating visually, as well as their ability to tune into shared aesthetic tastes and subjectivities. This form of subjectivity has deep roots in certain narratives of modernity itself where the tactile and the visual merge. How has this new *kósmoi*, this new order, been brought into being? And how have these new subjectivities been constructed?

Image and Subject

A series of photomontages made by László Moholy-Nagy illustrates perhaps the intimate relationship between image, touch, materials and subjectivity as a central project of modernity. In 1925, Moholy-Nagy took a photograph of Marcel Breuer with his hands up, facing the photographic lens, as if he were trying to stop the photographer himself in front of what arises behind: the architecture (fig. 4). Breuer's hands, open to the observer, presented a subjective counterpoint to the impersonal mechanism in front of him. Breuer's cautious and protective position appears as antagonistic to the growing interest Moholy-Nagy had developed since the early 1920s in the means of reproduction. The most economical gesture—trigger activation by the photographer's finger—will produce the most significant effects, once captured on the smooth surface of the pho-

Fig. 4

Fig. 5

Fig. 6

tographic film. With that same photograph, Moholy-Nagy made a photomontage that same year entitled *Das Gesetz der Serie* [The law of the series] (fig. 5). The compositional motif was none other than Breuer's own image, dissociated this time from its urban context. In it, Moholy-Nagy repeats, speculatively arranges and transforms the image into a composition of different grey scales, creating continuity through their overlap. Emerging from a circle—perhaps a reminder of the photographic origin—two curved lines converge to the right of the composition, cross the repetition of Breuer's figure, and indicate a path or direction to follow. The prescriptive or normative nature of this photomontage arises from the simultaneous use of the same element—with its variations and repetitions—in the same composition.

Certainly, *Das Gesetz der Serie* emphasizes the topic of modernity as repetition and variation of standards, be they mechanical or organic. [3] Moholy-Nagy wrote in 1929 that repetition and series were the way in which modern man recognized the aesthetic potential of technical progress and noted their subjective possibilities. [4] For Moholy-Nagy, the technical repetition of motifs did not belong to the family of ornamental geometric shapes of the past, but was the result of new expressive modes that emerged at the intersection between the modern subject and the technical and mechanical (re)production. It is here that he highlights photography as an instrument of vision capable of managing the "rhythmic play of light" for the benefit of the new aesthetic expressions of the modern subject. [5] Photography is both a visual and perceptual manner and a remote way to materialize and physically alter the world. His photographic series were, then, more than snapshots of these new scenes of modernity and became authentic abstract constructive elements of a superior aesthetic idea. The photographic process provided continuity and structure at the same time. Moholy-Nagy treated the images of his series as building blocks, and, as a result, photography integrated mechanical reproduction into organic assembly. [6]

Fig. 7

Fig. 8

3
In 1908, the art historian Wilhelm Worringer advocated for geometrical style in ornamentation in his epoch-making book *Abstraktion und Einfühlung*. Following Theodor Lipps and arguing against Heinrich Wölfflin, Worringer distinguished between ornamental regularity [*Regelmäßigkeit*] and lawfulness [*Gesetzmäßigkeit*], associating the former with the principle of empathy and the latter to the principle of abstraction. According to the German art historian, appreciating regularity depended on the subject, whereas lawfulness went beyond the individual, indicating a close relation with the external natural world. Lawfulness was a universal value, reconvening with the original sense of the word cosmos, or order. Moholy-Nagy frequently used hands, flowers and spirals in his photographs as organic counterpoints to the new medium. Worringer, Wilhem, *Abstraction and Empathy. A Contribution to the Psychology of Style* [1908], International Universities Press, New York, 1953, translated by Michael Bullock.

4
Moholy-Nagy, Láslzó, *Von Material zu Architektur*, A. Langen, Munich, 1929, p. 70.

5
Moholy-Nagy, Lászlő, "A New Instrument of Vision", *Telehor, The International Review for the New Vision*, No. 1, 1936; republished in Gruber, Klemens and Botar, Oliver A. I. (eds.), *Telehor, L. Moholy-Nagy*, Lars Müller Publishers, Zurich, 2011, p. 36. Also in Kostelanetz, Richard (ed.), *Moholy-Nagy*, Praeger Publishers, New York/Washington, 1970, pp. 50–53, translated by F. D. Klingender and P. Morton Shand.

6
Ibid.

There is no more surprising, yet, in its naturalness and organic sequence, simpler form than the photographic series. *This is the logical culmination of photography*. The series is no longer a "picture", and none of the canons of pictorial aesthetics can be applied to it. Here the separate picture loses its identity as such and becomes a detail of assembly, an essential structural element of the whole which is the thing itself. In this concatenation of its separate but inseparable parts a photographic series inspired by definite purpose can become at once the most potent weapon and the tenderest lyric.[7]

Moholy-Nagy continued to make use of Breuer's image for other photomontages and collages in later years. The most significant was perhaps one entitled *The Transformation*, where Breuer forms a kind of frieze with small variations (fig. 6). In the repetition on the right, Breuer's eyes have become feminized, replaced by the reverse of the seductive gaze of actress Gloria Swanson. Neither the feminization of vision nor the inversion of the gaze can be overlooked here in view of the architectural changes that were to come. Postwar architecture was to pay much more attention to details, ornaments, textures, lattices, etc., as a way to soften the aesthetic rigours with which the modern movement came to be identified. Nor can a subsequent montage be ignored—this time on request—in which the image of Breuer is used rhetorically for commercial purposes. *Halt! Waren Sie schon im Kaufhaus Schocken* is part of a commission for the German department store chain Schocken (fig. 7). In these two compositions, the use of the figure of Breuer links the seductive aspects with the purely economic ones in what was to be a preview of the postwar issues: consumerism and materialism. That Breuer's photo was significant in his career is shown by the repetition of the same gesture fifty years later (fig. 8), where the pose summarizes the way he treated the materials as a designer and architect, with his subjectivity always mediating the correspondence between manual and industrial work.[8]

Fig. 9

Fig. 10

Fig. 11

Turning now to architecture, two other photographs illustrate this formal transition between modern avant-garde and postwar architecture, in particular the relationship between Moholy-Nagy's photography and Breuer's architecture. The first of these images belongs to the design and construction of the US Embassy in The Hague (fig. 9).[9] Together with the elevations, perspectives and images of the work, this photograph helps us understand the building once opened. In it, we can intuit the pattern of light and shadow created by the hexagonal composition of glass and polished granite, set back slightly from the continuous limestone finish, a strategy similar to that used by Breuer in De Bijenkorf department store in Rotterdam (fig. 10). The choice of polished granite reinforces the idea of continuity of the reflection within a distorted hexagon of a higher order and brings to life the vitreous, crystalline quality that the perspectives created by the Breuer office promised. There is, however, something surprising in this photograph: the contrast of the abstract volumes with the ornate balcony from which the image was taken. The juxtaposition of a cast-iron pattern and architecture brings to mind another image taken by Moholy-Nagy in Marseille three decades earlier (fig. 11). Here, Moholy-Nagy placed the camera behind a similar pattern that illustrates the fascination of 1920s photography for plant motifs, especially in the work of Karl Blossfeldt.[10] However, despite these biological comparisons, Moholy-Nagy here reinforces the influence of photography on architecture, describing the balustrade as a necessary element "to separate the scene into individual cells through which their spatial quality is more emphasized".[11] For Moholy-Nagy, patterns were not merely cosmetic techniques, but frames responsible for a spatiality that a flat and continuous surface could not achieve.

By the end of the 1950s, the use and interpenetration of lattices, patterns and textures were common in the composition of façades, making the vision of photographic detail that Moholy-Nagy had suggested a real-

Fig. 12

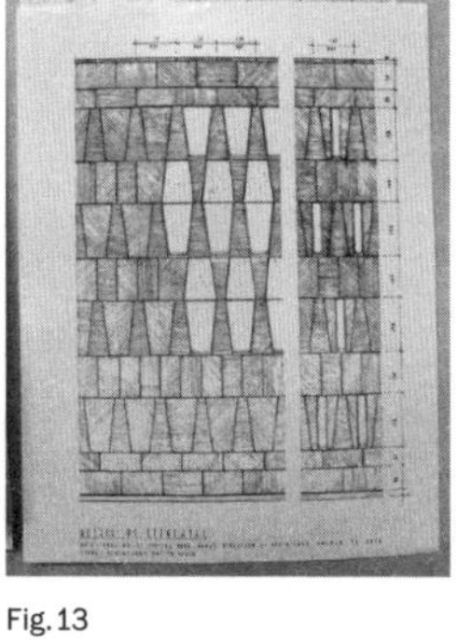

Fig. 13

7
Ibid.

8
The image belongs to the Bauhaus Archive in Berlin, and appears at the end of the monograph on Breuer edited by Isabelle Hyman, *Marcel Breuer, Architect: The Career and the Buildings*, N. H. Abrahams, New York, 2001.

9
Although it is not attributed, there are similar photographs that appear to indicate the photographer was Jan Versnel. On the work of Versnel, see: De Boer, Solange and Klose, Maarten, *Monografieen van Nederlandse Fotografen, Jan Versnel, onder redactie van Flip Bool*, Uitgeverij, Amsterdam, 1997.

10
I would like to thank Professor Spyros Papapetros for this reference. Alla Vronskaya has problematized the relation between Blossfeldt's *Urformen der Kunst* (1928) and nature, associating the volume with the work of Blossfeldt's former teacher and colleague Moritz Meurer, tracing back his influences to ornamental treatises such as Owen Jones's *The Grammar of Ornament* (1856).

11
Moholy-Nagy, László, "Space-Time and the Photographer", *The American Annual of Photography*, No. 57, Boston/London, 1943.

ity. The façades of the Breuer buildings acted just as Moholy-Nagy's photographs anticipated, proposing a new aesthetic in the last phase of the modern movement (fig. 12). Horizontal, vertical and diagonal lines populate the limestone frontage as indicators of the synthesis between manual design and industrial mechanical capacity. These textures help to make the play of contrast between light and shadow in the façade more present (fig. 13). The finished material result is anticipated by the artist's hand without any relation to the organization of the building, isolated as a constructive component and treated as an image: the material is previously scratched on the drawing board to build a mechanically scarified surface. The abstract and ornamental quality of hand drawing—a combination of geometric pattern and texture—already takes into account the mechanical capacity of production. As Adolf Loos suspected, the drawing board encourages the production of ornament, turning the architect into a graphic artist, a decorator who performs a superficial task of laceration. This is a material work designed to be seen, but in no case caressed.

Image Acts

Just as Breuer's materiality was defined in line with the photographic universe that surrounded him, the images that are generated today in studios or *a posteriori* contribute to the construction of specific material identities. The dominant visual culture has managed to subordinate the technical and programmatic aspects—fundamental aspects in the development of the architecture of the late twentieth century—to be used in favour of a two-dimensional compositional space where material, context and architectural elements have their place as long as they accept their unique image condition. It would seem that the photographers of the Düsseldorf School (Hilla and Bernd Becher, Andrea Gursky, Thomas Ruff, etc.), systematic and evocative in their representation of the world, had managed to impose

Fig. 14

a visual and material agenda on architecture, helped by the wide offer of images available on the internet (figs. 14–15). An example of this operating mode is the series in A5 format that Bas Princen used as a visual universe prior to his photographic work—as in the case of *Ringroad (Houston)*, 2005—and that had its impact on the early works of Kersten Geers and David van Severen.[12] The harmony between architect and photographer was, and continues to be, a constant in the development of the architectural avant-garde. There is today more than ever a shared visual order that is transmitted almost by direct osmosis between architects and architectural photographers. This order is mainly based on visual compositional exercises, a sign that the architect's vision increasingly specializes in the composition of form and matter.[13] There is a tectonics of the image itself that no current architect overlooks: architects and photographers alike understand their discipline as the ability to establish affective and effective relations between eye, space and touch. It is in the technical capacity to visualize the senses that subjectivities are handled today: transient and often ephemeral subjectivities, but an accurate expression of contemporary culture, where the hand sees and the eye touches.

Therefore, current materiality is no longer perceived as such unless it is visually tactile and digitally manipulable. To this end, it had to be dematerialized and recoded at origin. The haptic perception of the image provides the necessary dose of reality: stains, textures, the passage of time, imperfections and defects make it plausible. But also the lack of all these incidents, selectively framed, contrasted and transformed, pictorializes the image itself. The work of the Swedish photographer Jeanette Hägglund is an example of how a specific visual aesthetic transports us to alternative universes—to those *kósmoi* I referred to at the beginning (fig. 16). These images allow us to intuit a different social, cultural and political life, perhaps more hedonistic, more curated and compositional, but certainly an alternative to the existing one. The Bildbauten or Capriccio series by Philipp Schaerer or the imagined architectures of Filip Dujardin point in

Fig. 15

Fig. 16

Fig. 17

12
Norwood, Vanessa (ed.), *The Construction of an Image: Bas Princen*, Bedford Press, London, 2016.

13
See: Wirz, Heinz (ed.), *architecten de vylder vinck taillieu*, Quart Verlag, Lucerne, 2016.

the same direction: the need to represent fictional realities is facilitated by a digital cosmetic where the usual and the surprising, the feasible and the unlikely, merge (fig. 17). They are tangible yet delocalized spaces that promote a presence that is worldly and perhaps more aesthetic, but as prescriptive as it is evocative.

The generation of present-day architects—illustrated by the work of the Barozzi/Veiga and Baukunst + Bruther studios included in this block—has built its aesthetic and material identities in parallel to the visual development generated by its spaces (figs. 18–19). The space produces and reproduces, influencing in turn architecture's capacity to change like an *opera aperta*, without renouncing its operability. Adrien Verschuere underlines the influence on Baukunst's work of the idea of the "speech act" by the British philosopher of language John Austin, according to which the function of speech is to establish or anticipate certain actions and make them effective. Examples of speech acts for Austin are weddings and baptisms, where certain phrases or utterances anticipate reality and establish a new order between subjects. Similarly, the projective images that architects generate with their spaces maintain confidence in the transformative capacity of architecture. The work of Maxim Delvaux (Baukunst + Bruther) and Jesús Arenas and Simon Menges (Barozzi/Veiga) contributes both to the generation of a new aesthetic and to the construction of that new relational order that is transmitted both physically and digitally. Once constructed, the image strives to become a photographic or iconic act, to use the expressions of Phillipe Dubois (*acte photographique*) or Horst Bredekamp (*Bildakts*): images that architects expect to acquire a degree of life in themselves as agents of change.[14] The image is animated in the subject and prompts new forms of action and occupation of the space. Unlike previous examples in modernity—Mies van der Rohe's work comes to mind—the digital world brings with it a certain architectural "photographism": a hope that the manipulated and finished image effects its rhetorical capabilities beyond the physical limits of the represented

Fig. 18

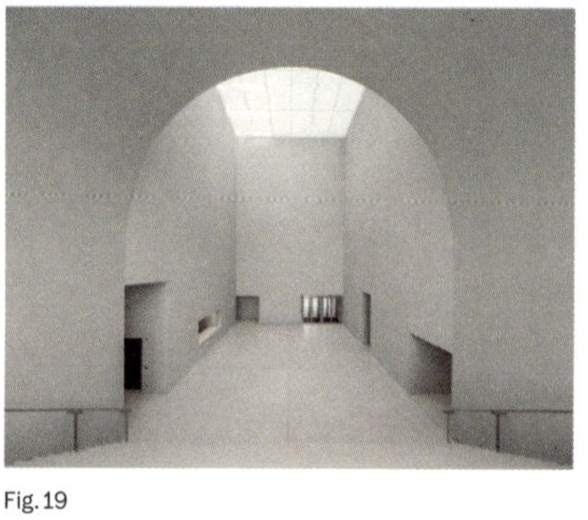

Fig. 19

object.[15] It is this rhetoric that permeates the new cosmetic of today's architectural image.

Thus, the image *is* an act, as Henri Lefebvre reminded us in his *Critique of Everyday Life*, an essential communicative and social act in the definition of contemporary culture. That the act of projecting is an act of imagining and anticipating the possible effects of architecture is nothing new. Likewise that the architectural image itself becomes the place of anticipated technical work.[16] But present-day techniques and technologies are certainly transforming the way and the forms in which the ghosts of the past come to life. The economy of the image today means standing out from the rest through the singularization of multiple architectural fragments, whether these are tectonic or structural details, or existing or contextual elements. It is the past in the form of memory and context which contributes and constantly put forward as an aesthetic tactic that is, above all, a tactic for survival.

14
Dubois, Philippe, *L'Acte photographique et autres essais*, Armand Colin, Paris, 1990; Bredekamp, Horst, *Theorie des Bildakts: über das Lebensrecht des Bildes*, Suhrkamp Verlag, Frankfurt, 2011.

15
Zimmerman, Claire, *Photographic Architecture in the Twentieth Century*, University of Minnesota Press, Minneapolis, 2014. On the topic of photographism, see Schnaith, Nelly, *Lo visible y lo invisible en la imagen fotográfica*, La Oficina, Madrid, 2011.

16
Levine, Neil, *Modern Architecture: Representation and Reality*, Yale University Press, New Haven, 2010.

Mark Pimlott

All the World's a Stage: Artifice and Fiction in the Public Interior

As an urban citizen, one should be concerned with one's freedom: the freedom to occupy space, to be in the world, to feel as though one can have agency within one's circumstances; to move, to act, to be oneself in public among others one does not know. This freedom, or the illusion of this freedom, is articulated within the city's interior. The city is a phenomenon that spreads everywhere, even into nature itself. It creates a condition of distinct character. In Italy before its unification in the nineteenth century, that character could be seen in social behaviour, dress, laws and ways of building. The province and the city constituted an interior, one of agreement or acquiescence. Although the city-state no longer exists, a condition of interior persists regardless. In the late eighteenth century, Thomas Jefferson's experiment of transforming the American continental territory into a completely claimed "interior" was achieved through a regulatory

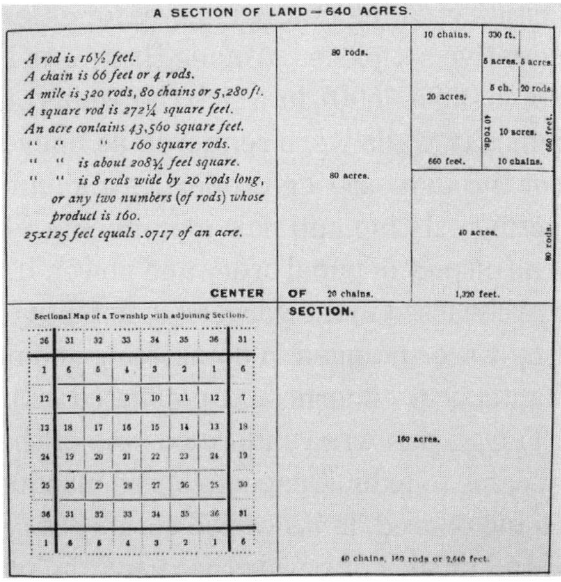

and operative device: a grid, that was deployed through documentary, geological and military surveys that led to the elimination of indigenous populations—the other—and the rendering of their world into an interior beholden to the ideology of self-realization.[1]

It is not difficult to see that the constructed environment is thoroughly urbanized. Attendant upon this condition are myriad structures and infrastructures that bind buildings to streets, urban centres to regional territories and people to all of these in arrangements that affect behaviour, producing the urban subject and their subjectivity, determining the relations of these subjects not only to each other but to authority and its imperatives. The condition is all-consuming: nature is co-opted as a representational figure that serves as a foil and enhancement to the completeness of an interior. The city is everywhere, and so too is its maintenance of behavioural order, its aura of consent. It is proposed as a total environment. *Urbanización* as imagined by Ildefons Cerdà in 1867[2] posited the

1
Mark Pimlott: *Without and Within: Essays on Territory and the Interior* (Rotterdam: Episode publishers, 2007).

2
Ildefons Cerdà: *Teoría general de urbanización* (1867). See discussion by Ross Exo Adams, *Circulation & Urbanization* (London: SAGE, 2019).

spread of the city over the entire world, rendering countryside and city as one: a territorial condition of "the urban" that would shape the behaviour of its occupants. The political significance is evident, and consistent with the ideological bases for Jefferson's Land Ordinance in the United States (1785)[3] and Baron Georges-Eugène Haussmann's transformations of the administrative and built structures of Paris (1850–1873), directed towards the condition of an interior. The transformation of Barcelona itself following Cerdá's plan (1859) is a design both of the city's form and the citizen as urban subject.

These propositions, which in their ideal states constituted territorial urbanized environments, were preceded by the many urban designs of the Renaissance[4] and Baroque periods. Idealized figures assuming the forms of streets, squares and sequences were imposed upon the less visibly ordered fabrics of cities, creating new narratives for cities' spaces as scenes, replete with decorative set pieces. Among them was Pope Sixtus V's interventions in Rome (1585–1590), in which the skeins of pilgrimage routes within the ancient city walls were rendered as lines extended through open land and cut through existing properties and buildings, a geometry of streets connecting existing and new monuments,[5] built as settings of high artifice for the display of papal order and power. It was the urban version of a strategy rehearsed in the gardens of nobility, in which parterres, paths and planting were arranged in dominating geometrical schema; or in evocations of fantastical wildernesses, populated with allegorical figures and structures. The garden was rendered a kind of theatre, and the city, correspondingly, came to exhibit aspects of the masque.[6]

Sixtus V's Rome offered, in its varied set pieces and their incidents, highly concentrated images of power that used the entire city as a field or scaffold for its representations. Similarly, the image of Haussmann's Paris, one of administrative, functional and behavioural control, was diffused through the entire urban structure, its infrastructure, equipment and appearances. These environments, which tended to the condition of an interior, were artificial: they relied upon artifice to give form to their ideas and their fictions. They were contrived to achieve an objective, to define or form the urban subject for purposes of predictable behaviour or performance through prescribed forms, patterns and imagery. They both formed the subject and influenced subjectivities, offering little space for the subject's agency beyond obeisance.

In contemporary corporate, retail, cultural, institutional or lifestyle environments,[7] architecture's appearances are employed to simultaneously display and mask power, and to affect subjects' behaviour in relation to that power through prescription, inculcation and deception. Within such staged settings, however, there is always the possibility that the fictions that reside within them might be understood precisely as fictions rather than realities, and that they might be rendered vulnerable to the interpretations and subjectivities of the urban subject. Making the arrangements, forms and imagery of the city—as constructs of ideology or power—available to the subject's consciousness should be central to the architect's considerations of the architecture of the city and its condition as an interior. As the architect is directly involved in the construction of the city, so too is the architect involved in the construction of its fictions, which might be turned towards creating scenes of actual freedoms for the urban subject.

If one can speak of a condition of an interior, then there are spaces in which the fictions within that condition are especially concentrated. Public interiors are those spaces in the urbanized environment where ideas are displayed and directed toward the public, or publics. These are spaces in which urban subjects are particularly conscious of themselves as part of a public, regardless of the nature of that space's ownership. In this way, a state museum, a shopping mall, an airport, a library and a market hall are all public interiors.[8] Giving one's attention to the history of such interiors, one will understand them as spaces of relations, effects and artifice. They are, by nature, acutely artificial. Their appearances are laden with fictive narratives about what they are, who they are for and how they are to be experienced. They have developed from coercion at an intimate scale to their current, seamless connection to a worldwide, technologically-driven, infrastructural condition of an interior.[9] Their artifice is geared towards effects meant to achieve agreement and predictable behaviour, to sugarcoat the pill of obeisance, inevitably toward the reinforcement of power, bolstered by consumption. What might counteract these negative characteristics? What might produce, in contrast, spaces for the subjective imagination and its freedoms? The answers may reside within artifice itself.

Through artifice, ideas are given form so that they might appear. Artifice is necessary.[10] This does not mean that an idea is directly translated into appearance: something, appearance, must be an agent of the idea.

3
Catherine Maumi: *Thomas Jefferson et le project du Nouveau Monde* (Paris: Éditions de la Villette, 2007); Mark Pimlott, *op. cit.*

4
Leonardo Benevolo: *The Architecture of the Renaissance* (1968), 2 vols (London: Routledge & Kegan Paul, 1978).

5
Pier Vittorio Aureli: *The Possibility of an Absolute Architecture* (Cambridge MA: MIT Press, 2011).

6
The development of the British architect Inigo Jones (1573–1652) is an example. His designs for masques fused musings on the ruins of Rome that were the subject of academic study (Alberti) with the mystery of the garden in the form of architectural sets, constructed in gardens as background to entertainments; as ideas, they moved to the theatrical stage as scenery; from the stage, they became architectural propositions: see Jones's Queen's House, Greenwich (1616–1635) and Banqueting Hall in Whitehall, London (1619–1649).

7
New York's Hudson Yards development (2018) is a typical fusion of all these in one total environment, where user's engagement is encouraged, monitored and monetized.

8
Manuel de Solà-Morales, "Public Spaces, Collective Spaces" (1992), in Tom Avermaete, Klaske Havik, Hans Teerds (eds.): *Architectural Positions: Architecture, Modernity, and the Public Sphere* (Amsterdam: SUN, 2009), originally published in *La Vanguardia*, Barcelona.

9
Keller Easterling, *Extrastatecraft: The Power of Infrastructure Space* (London: Verso, 2014).

10
Joseph Rykwert: "The Necessity of Artifice" (1971), in *The Necessity of Artifice* (London: Academy Editions, 1982), pp. 58–59.

The agent, inevitably, loses something of its message along the way: there is a gap between the idea and its articulation, a lack that comes with the movement of idea towards appearance, the utterance towards form. In the notion at the core of the allegory of painting,[11] the representation of a loved one is rendered poignant by the limitations inherent within representation and artifice. The image holds something of its subject: the re-membering inscribed in the image strains to re-present the loved one, to make them present once more.

The outward forms or appearances of man-made artefacts are, at once, constructed facts and representations. In the case of architecture, internal arrangements and external appearances embody numerous narratives, stemming from the body from whom the commission originates and the architect who gives them form. These appearances can be of the order of direct communication: an *architecture parlante*; or they can be more subtle or complex. Ideas might be given outward appearances that provide a diversion or other narratives for the notions at their core. For example, power might be represented through appearances that may variously suggest an enchanted garden, or a ruin, or an efficient machine. The use of these suggestions by agents of a public interior's appearance would depend on their legibility to an intended "audience" or subject, one likely to be already culturally formed or inculcated. The subject within the interior is in the process of being formed.

It was the consideration of these possibilities, and the appearances and configurations that might represent objectives connected with the projection of ideas, such as control, reform or enfranchisement, that led to my proposal for students of architecture at TU Delft for study of the public interior not in terms of types, in the manner of Pevsner, or of technological development, in the manner of Giedion, or in terms of the university's traditions of plan analysis, but in terms of thematic and representational motifs inscribed in their outward appearances and the suggestions and possibilities latent within those appearances.[12] This acknowledged that these interiors were designed. It was evident that a large number of interiors across very different contexts and historical periods through to the present alluded to conditions, states or models that were independent of type, and that a language of appearances transcended type and found itself in use in a variety of representational and operational tasks.

The interiors could be shown to be vehicles for ideas, assuming forms that communicated those ideas through image, atmosphere and imposition. The subject experiencing these interiors was placed in the position of reading, interpreting and entering the fictions of those interiors' appearances and arrangements. In each instance, it was clear that the subject's experience was central to the architectural project and the object of its artifice. The subject was cast within its scenes as a figure who would be largely compelled to obey; yet it was also clear that the subject was at

11
Pablo Garcia: "The Origin of Painting", in Projection Systems, https://projectionsystems.wordpress.com/2009/09/06/the-origin-of-painting/ [accessed 2019 05 28].

12
The Fundamentals lectures at TU Delft in the Chair of Architecture of the Interior 2012–2014, became the basis of the author's book *The Public Interior as Idea and Project* (Heijningen: Jap Sam Books, 2016).

once a citizen, reader and interpreter. Students were therefore invited to consider the public interior neither as scientists, technicians, strategists, programmers nor apparatchiks, but as interpreters, so as to consciously see the artifice and staging of the public interiors of study. This was in the hope that the student thereafter—as a designer—would be able to engage with the fictional and subjective aspect of architecture (while maintaining concern with all its other aspects) so as to recast or propose new fictions for the imagination of experiencing subjects; and, in so doing, expand those conditions that might permit these subjects to pursue their ideas of freedom.

The course was developed into the book *The Public Interior as Idea and Project* (2016),[13] which proposed six themes that seemed to dominate the Western European tradition of the public interior: the garden, the palace, the ruin, the shed, the machine and the network. The first of these themes were allusive and reflective, suggestive of the condition of humankind, mortality, the lightness of being and the image of worldly power. The latter of the themes were indicative of the changes specific to the Enlightenment and modernity, such as those to the scale and scope of administration, the state, industrialization and the distribution of power. The impacts of industrialization, particularly on the organization of the city and its institutions, were keenly felt in the various appearances of the public interior, which attempted to diminish the disruptive forces of its effects by harnessing them, rendering their spaces alternately as palatable or as efficient as possible.

The "garden" alluded to the lost condition of Paradise and its apparent unity. It was invoked to describe the origins of both the condition of being interior (Paradise, a walled garden) and architecture itself, and was as potent for the design of Gothic cathedrals as it was for palatial rooms, such as the Silver Room at Amalienburg, the passages of early nineteenth-century Paris, the Crystal Palace, the Galleria Vittorio Emanuele II, Museums of Natural History in London, Oxford and Paris, *grands magasins* such as Au Bon Marché, American shopping malls, the Ford Foundation and Bürolandschaft.

The "palace" suggested a building that was both an accumulation of cells and a scaffold for representations, whose message and source would change alongside changes in the agency and nature of power. It was represented by real palaces such as the Winter Palace in St Petersburg with its succession of elaborate interiors as well as all those buildings that bent the palace as idea to their will, beginning with "public" museums such as Schinkel's Altes Museum, gentlemen's clubs in London, the Crystal Palace and the department stores that followed, as well as worker's clubs, *maisons des peuples* and peoples' palaces on both the left and right of the political spectrum, these all being co-opted, through the inspiration of Cedric Price's Fun Palace, into the museums and cultural centres of the latter part of the twentieth century.

The "ruin", quite apart from representing ruminations on the destiny of all constructs,[14] was also used to establish connections with and mastery of the past. From the scholarship of Alberti, which reclaimed Roman architecture for the use of Renaissance institutions, to that of James Stuart and Nicholas Revett, who, similarly, documented the neglected antiquities of Greece for British dilettantes in order to legitimate the ambitions of the British imperial project; from the cultural education and appropriations of the Grand Tours from the sixteenth to nineteenth centuries (yielding generations of amateurs besotted with ruins and Piranesi's *invenzioni capricciose di carceri*) to the ruin's various uses as scenery for a society's self-legitimation, whether using ambiguity (as in the case of Soane's Bank of England), or bombast (as in the case of McKim Mead and White's Penn Station in New York), the ruin has remained a remarkably resilient motif. Most recently, in Lacaton + Vassal's Palais de Tokyo, the ruin appears as a figure of disruption, play and freedom.

The "shed" appeared as an indication of the great and necessary measure of accommodation of goods, machines and people imposed by industrialized urbanization. As suitable for a market as small as those of *bastide* towns and as large as those of Les Halles Centrales, or for train stations such as the Gare du Nord, the shed—as idea—has also been deployed to shelter great expositions from Paris to Montréal, scenes of cultural and political gatherings such as those proposed by Mies van der Rohe and his acolytes, and environments of entertainment and consumption exemplified by mega-malls such as Jon Jerde's Mall of America. The shed continues to appear as a vital device for the diffuse metropolis, creating vast spaces without any apparent representational agenda, containing everything.

The "machine" was a product of the post-feudal State and its efforts towards the effective management of all aspects of its organization and its institutions, with particular emphasis on control of citizens' associations, health, behaviour and performance. As a motif, the machine has infiltrated

13
Mark Pimlott: *The Public Interior as Idea and Project* (Heijningen: Jap Sam Books, 2016).

14
Percy Bysshe Shelley: "Ozymandias" (1818); Georg Simmel, "The Ruin" (1911).

the architectural project, its methods and its education (from the École Polytechnique to the Beaux-arts to its descendants), to the workings of its plans (from those of institutions, to spaces of transport, consumption, and spectacle), and its language of representation (from orthodoxies of Neo-classicism to those of corporate modernism and mediated realities). The machine as a motif has proven particularly suited to its integration into the complex systems of the metropolis and provided its workings with imagery that reinforces its mythical narratives, from Garnier's Opéra to Grand Central Terminal and the Centre Pompidou.

Lastly, the book's chapter on the "network" described those public interiors most directly related to a condition of interior. From the bazaar to the arcades,[15] the indoor shopping mall as invented by Victor Gruen[16] to the infrastructural spaces of stations and airports, the deep interiors of Las Vegas casinos,[17] the speculations of structuralists typified by Candilis Josic Woods' Freie Universität and the endless spaces of continuous interiors bemoaned as "junkspace",[18] the network has been woven into existing contexts and their patterns, extending its own territories. It has, over time, surrendered imagery to other agents of artifice. The network has tended to the condition of a system and, like the palace before it, it has served as a scaffold for representations, media and spectacle.[19] It has ceded to the potentials of the liberation of movement, emulating the pattern of the street and proposing some kind of degraded ideal in its place, which, one must admit, is another kind of scenery.[20]

Within the context of this overview and discussions with students that followed, several projects arose that came to be regarded as models worthy of emulation. Each retained a measure of artifice, yet used their working fictions to enhance opportunities for interpretation, use, mis-use, appropriation, encounter, gathering, publicness, and, in their own ways, made themselves available for the exercise of freedoms. As though attentive to suggestions within Victor Horta's Maison du Peuple (1899), Owen Williams's Pioneer Health Centre (1936), Beaudouin, Lods and Prouvé's

Maison du Peuple (1938) and Cedric Price's Fun Palace (1964), a series of projects—Peter Celsing's Kulturhuset in Stockholm (1974), Piano and Rogers's Centre Georges Pompidou (1977), the Sandberg Wing of the Stedelijk Museum in Amsterdam (1967, destroyed), Frank van Klingeren's De Meerpaal (1967) in Dronten and 't Karregat (1971) in Eindhoven (both radically altered), Lina Bo Bardi's MASP (1969), SESC Pompéia (1978) and her Teatro Oficina (1984) in Sao Paulo—proposed truly public interiors, in which the public had agency. Furthermore, they were more than abstract vehicles awaiting life; they were frameworks for, variously, the fictions within the garden, the palace, the ruin, the shed and the machine, offered as scenery for appropriation by an emancipated public. Parallels today can be seen in the projects of Lacaton + Vassal and their generous spatial provisions; in the allusions to ruins and temples in Herzog & de Meuron's 1111 Lincoln Road in Miami (2010); in the reconciliations with time in the courtyard of Flores y Prats's Casal Balaguer in Palma de Mallorca (2018); and in the public room of the Stadhal/Markthal of Robbrecht en Daem and Marie Josee Van Hee in Ghent (2012). All enable the possibility of people assuming their places in public, in scenes made for their own uses and imaginations. All seem to point in a direction that evokes the condition nurtured by the English theatre director Peter Brook,[21] which would have the public interior as an "empty space": a stage for actors and the audience, all together in their own play.

15
Johann Friedrich Geist: *Passagen: Ein Bautyp des 19. Jahrhunderts* (1969) (München: Prestel Verlag, 1982).

16
Victor Gruen, Larry Smith: *Shopping Towns USA* (New York: New York, 1960).

17
Robert Venturi, Denise Scott-Brown, Steven Izenour: *Learning from Las Vegas: The Forgotten Symbolism of Architectural Form* (revised edition) (Cambridge MA: MIT Press, 1977).

18
Marc Augé: *Non-Places: Introduction to an Anthropology of Supermodernity* (1992), transl. John Howe (London, New York: Verso, 1995).

19
Guy Debord, transl. David Nicholson-Smith, *The Society of the Spectacle* (1968) (New York: Zone Books, 1995).

20
Rem Koolhaas, "Junkspace", in Nobuyuki Yoshida [ed.], Rem Koolhaas, *OMA@work: Architecture and Urbanism*, May 2000 Special Issue (Tokyo: A+U Publishing, 2000).

21
Peter Brooke, *The Empty Space* (London: Penguin, 1968).

Next, we have two parallelepiped buildings with occasional external extensions in the form of a pre-existing fragment or a communication core, in both cases defining their architectural personality. MCBA is located in the centre of Lausanne in an urban fragment undergoing transformation, while FRAME stands in an empty plot at the eastern limit of Brussels. The first is already built, while the second is, for the moment, a virtual project. The urban vocation of these two projects requires the MCBA to organize, together with another two museums, a fragment of empty and full spaces at a tangent to the railway tracks, and the FRAME to reconstitute a peripheral site to become advertisement and city, thanks to its transparent nature. In the MCBA, the relation of the public interior with the urban exterior is hermetic due to the strict programmatic requirements of an art museum, but without relinquishing exceptional and strategic transparencies. In the FRAME, the definition of its four façades is personalized in a more fragmented way, reacting to the diverse and specific stimuli of the context. In the confrontation of these two buildings, materiality offers a play of opposites. The massive nature of the MCBA contrasts with the FRAME, built with the double reflective skins of a building that is infrastructural in nature.

Barozzi/Veiga
MUSÉE CANTONAL DES BEAUX-ARTS (MCBA), Lausanne, 2008–2018

In 2011 Barozzi/Veiga won the international competition for the master plan of the new art district in Lausanne, Switzerland—Platform 10—and the design of the Fine Arts Museum. Located in the city centre, the project proposed a master plan for the city's three main museums: the Museum of Fine Arts MCBA, the Museum of Contemporary Design and Applied Arts MUDAC, and the Photography Museum Musée de l'Elysée. The site, of more than 2 ha near the central train station, was mostly occupied by an old nineteenth-century train shed and some other industrial buildings.

As an urban strategy, the projects introduce a new structuring void, a new public plaza around which the museums gravitate. The void stretches along the site and integrates the buildings into the scale of the city fabric and, by connecting to the existing train station concourse, places them in continuity with the city's public space. The architecture becomes the frame for the urban life of the city, the container of the new public plaza.

The new Museum of Fine Arts is situated on the site's southern edge as a longitudinal monolithic volume, parallel to the train tracks. Like the train station, it defines an urban space while protecting it from the nuisance of the trains. Embracing this condition, the Museum of Fine Arts, the biggest of the three museums, carries and expresses the memory of the site, echoing its former industrial character with pragmatic forms, rigorous geometry, and hard, sharp lines. The MCBA is specific to its site; it tries to establish a link with a certain atmosphere, to anchor it in the city in both space and history.

The opportunity to create an urban void led to the demolition of part of the existing train shed. However, the preservation of the memory of a place is achieved through the preservation of fragments. The project preserves part of the original hall and transforms it into a central piece of the project. In a very classical relationship, the new building of the MCBA acts as a backdrop, highlighting the presence of the old arched window as a fragment, a protuberance, and main protagonist of the building from the train tracks.

The overall building is relatively hermetic to protect the museum collections and therefore has a closed, introverted façade on the track side, in the south, and a more open, permeable, animated façade in the north.

The ground floor was developed as an extension of the public plaza and thus houses the main social programmes of the café, bookshop, entrance, auditoriums etc. Once inside the foyer, the saved fragment reveals its full role as a substantial structuring component of the new MCBA. Here the carved arch resonates with the tranquil, double-height space of the foyer and connects it with the view of the train tracks. It also structures the architectural programme, organizing the main circulation to the upper floors, and separating the permanent and temporary exhibitions.

The complexity of the programme is solved in a very simple and synthetic way, as five cores structure the brief at every level but also help as structural constructive elements that contain the form of the building.

The upper floor is bathed in natural light coming from modular trapezoidal skylights facing north, diffusing the light and offering optimal lighting conditions for the art.

The museum is organized on three floors connected by the continuous void of the foyer that gives structure to the circulation. The exhibition spaces are situated on the higher levels, on both sides of the foyer. The permanent gallery in the east is separated from the temporary gallery in the west, and can be visited jointly or in parallel thanks to independent vertical circulation, allowing future comprehensive exhibitions as well as smaller capsule collections. The connection in the permanent exhibition is conceived as a social and event space, a staircase as an auditorium for smaller lectures or inaugurations.

The longitudinal façades of the MCBA are the most representative ones. The north façade's light exposure is minimized by deep vertical fins between which are large, tall windows. The fins are designed to prevent direct sunlight from ever entering the light-sensitive zones of the building.

The brick façades evoke the industrial history of the site and offer a texture, a vibrant pattern to the monolith. On the plaza, the spatial rhythm of the vertical window fins breaks up the massiveness of the monolith and reveals the openings. At night, the fins serve as a canvas to diffuse the light coming from the museum, transforming the façade on the plaza.

The founding idea of the plazas' urban design is to create an exterior public space in dialogue with the museums. Like the buildings, it integrates fragments of its industrial past: the train tracks and the turning plate. Some tall trees will also be planted in order to reinforce its place in the public space continuum with the train station plaza.

Second floor

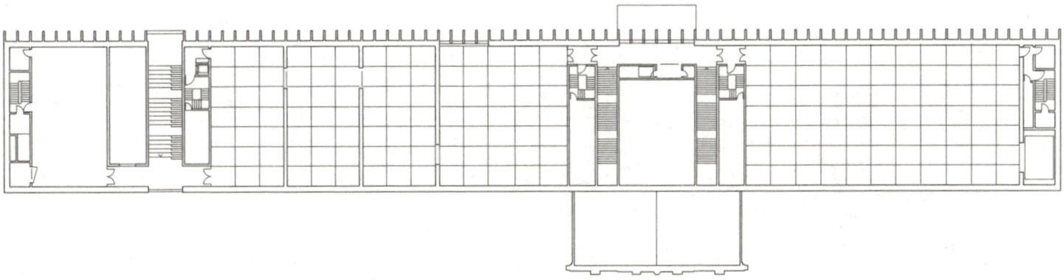

First floor

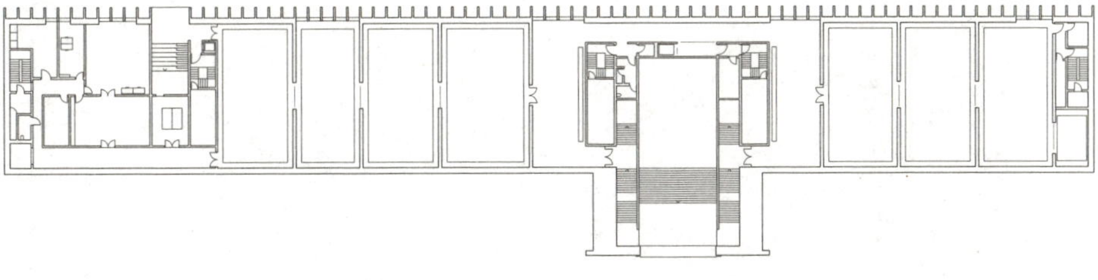

Orlati
Orlati
Orlati

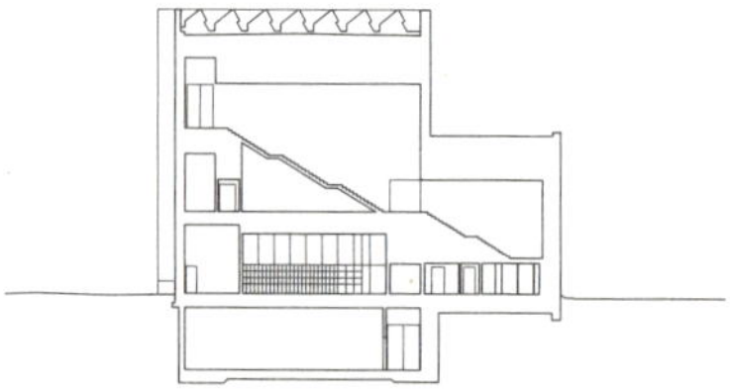

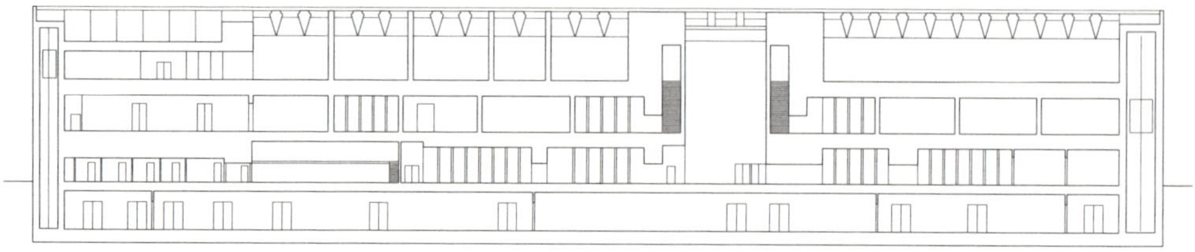

Baukunst & Bruther
FRAME, Brussels, 2017 (under construction)

East of central Brussels, opposite one of the motorways leading out of the city and the six-lane Reyers Boulevard, the project for a future Médiapark, initiated by the city, aims to redefine and revitalize the district. At the southern end of this urban redevelopment area, which will host an innovative media ecosystem, is a plot allocated to the Maison des Médias, to the north of which is the building. Unitary and compact, it rises 33.30 m on five floors plus two mezzanines—one below grade on the ground floor and another above the fifth floor—a walk-on terrace on the sixth floor.

The different treatment of the four façades reflects the desire to turn the building towards its context. First, the south façade unfolds like a billboard, creating a link with the programme and addressing a vast horizon. It thus contrasts with the verticality of the gabled faces, overlooking the long perspective of Colonel Bourg Street on the east side and the buildings on Reyers Boulevard to the west. This desire to open up to the city is accentuated by two notable features: on the one hand, the double-height hall, which extends the public space to the south via a view and thus transforms the building into a belvedere with a panoramic vista of central Brussels.

Programmatic constraints, accentuated by the need for cohabitation between partners, led to a project based on intense spatial rationality. Structural design was at the heart of the concern to achieve the necessary flexibility.

The functions are distributed across activity floors of roughly 1,000 m^2—15.00×67.50 m—superimposed across an entirely open floor plan. Their dimensions ensure natural lighting, through views and a good balance between mixed uses (either in an open-space configuration or in more clearly differentiated areas). Indeed, although the building's occupation can be largely reconfigured, the specific brief oriented the volumetric choices. For example, studios requiring significant ceiling heights triggered the decision to double the height on the fifth floor with mezzanines, giving it the status of an almost distinct element from the rest of the building while contributing to the typological richness of the whole.

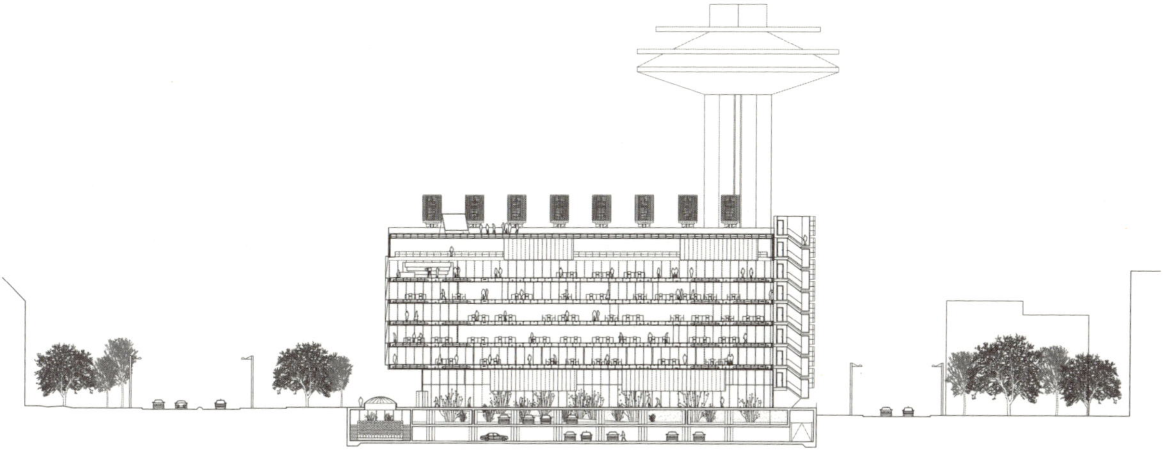

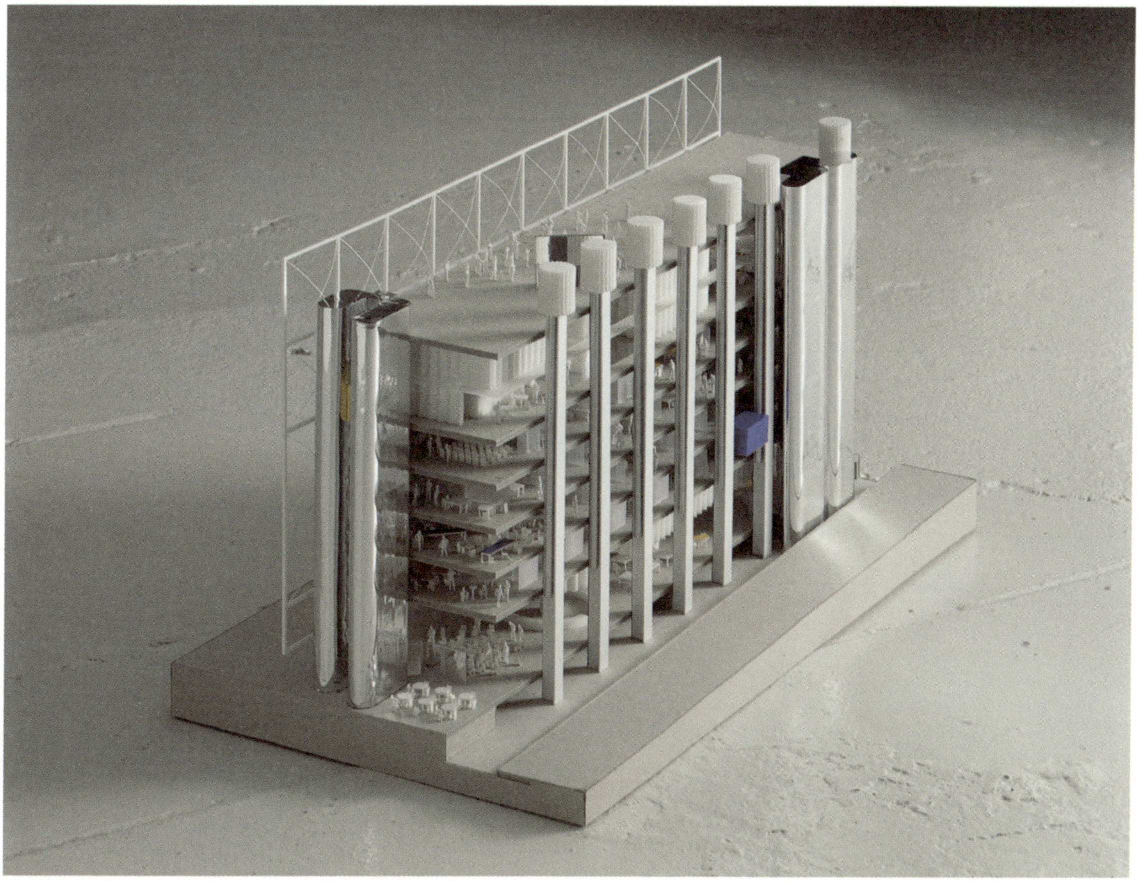

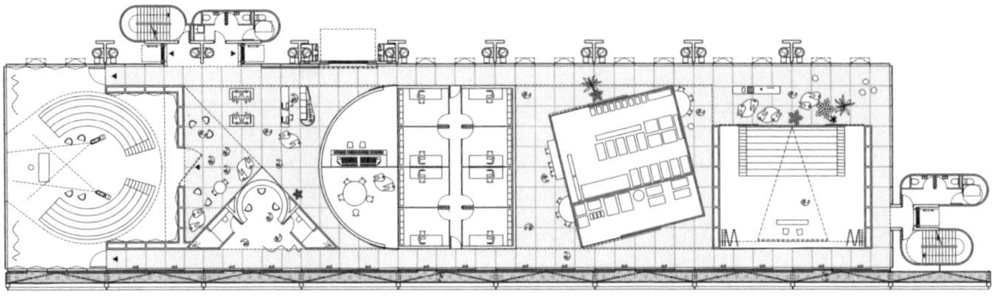

Fifth floor

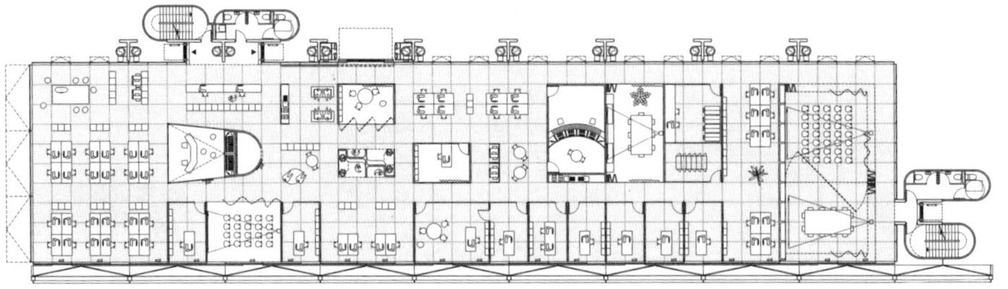

Fourth floor

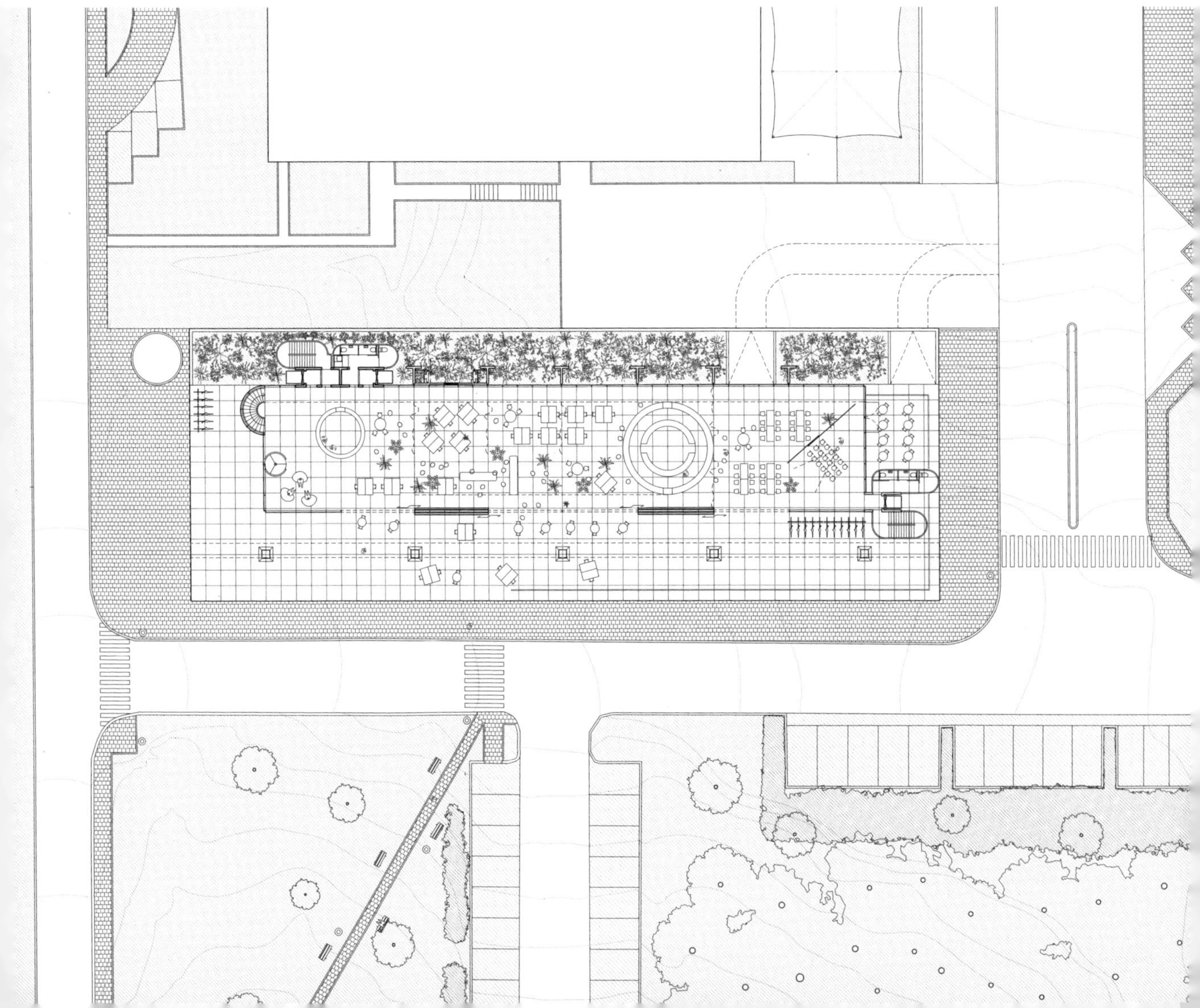

What I see when I look at...

While browsing the website of one of the co-authors of the FRAME building in Brussels, we became aware of an unsettling situation: the images of apparently static buildings and cities suddenly come to life. A flock of birds takes flight in the middle of a square, the tops of the trees sway gently from the effect of the wind; a surface of water ripples due to the effects of the breeze; a procession of cars, trucks and people circulates with deliberation along a great avenue; curtains wave without any human presence involved. We are unable to say whether the architectures that we have just witnessed are real or virtual. But we know for sure that some are and others are not. We wonder what there could be between the leaves of the real trees in motion and the virtual curtain wall that reflects an urban mirage.

(directors' note)

The Piece and the Entirety
Scale 3

The observation and examination of the constructive detail is a characteristic exercise of our time: the zoom as identification of the whole. Construction detail is understood here as a unit that conceptually supports an architectural fragment.[1] This third section therefore reviews the evolution of the field of construction over the last decades and, with it, the ability of the architectural fragment (the piece) to explain the nature and identity of the entirety. Again in the European context, it addresses systems and construction materialities at the service of cosmetic techniques, again confronting the regionalist and local with industrialized and globalized techniques—in short, a new version of the debate between subjectivity and objectivity, on the basis of the definition of an expanded materiality.

The study of the fragment reveals that the discipline today simultaneously explores a new materiality, revises known materials, integrates new techniques and, in particular, reviews the link between humankind and architecture, and that of both with the climate and environmental balance. Past and present become available for the articulation of languages, of moments, with few concessions to utopia.

This section also includes "three-dimensional poems", a contribution from the field of contemporary art with a poetic and rational, almost scientific, vocation, where "matter is the hinge between the mental and the physical".

1
FONTCUBERTA, Joan: "Estética de la fragmentación. Ruidos de archivo", *La cámara de Pandora. La fotografía después de la fotografía*, Gustavo Gili, Barcelona, 2012.

Javier García-Germán
Miquel Rodríguez

An Expanded Materiality

During the last few decades building technology has oscillated—among other lines—between the paths traced by Reyner Banham's *Theory and Design in the First Machine Age* (1960) and *The Architecture of the Well-Tempered Environment* (1969) and, years later, by Kenneth Frampton's *Studies in Tectonic Culture* (1995). These books have succeeded in framing the scope of technological understanding within architectural culture for the last few years. While Banham championed technological progress and studied how new building technologies—specifically mechanical climate-control technology—were transforming orthodox architectural parameters, Frampton's critical regionalism, a reaction to generic global modern technologies, insisted on architecture's connection to place and local technology, and the mechanical gravitational nature of its tectonics.

Interestingly these two lines of thought have proved to a large extent to be right. On the one hand, as Banham noted, there has been a strong move towards industrial production and standardization which has attuned materials and building systems to a worldwide manufacturing network. This has been paralleled by a tendency towards an oppressive building regulation framework. These two questions have propelled prefabrication, specialization of components and non-qualified assembly in an uncritical way. This trend has been biased—spurred by sustainability and climate change—by a growing interest in zero-energy buildings, which has motivated a shift towards insulated and airtight envelopes and efficient mechanical systems, directing industrialized building systems towards thermodynamics. This move towards industrialization and energy efficiency is offset by a symmetrical and opposite tendency—championed by Frampton's critical regionalism—towards local traditions and technologies.

Overriding the building industries' material inertias, this essay presents five perspectives that shed light on a more promising material approach, attuned not only to ecological and social demands, but also to human desires for health and comfort, promising a built environment of ecological emancipation and sensorial intensity.

In contrast to the market-driven global mainstream building practices, *material atmospheres* explores a material culture specific to a place and climate. If building materials are connected to climatic performance, the technological choice depends on an array of questions such as weight, porosity, colour, etc., which not only have thermodynamic implications—conductivity, thermal inertia or reflectivity—but also, more importantly, architectural qualities. Furthermore the choice of materials is complemented by material assembly, as there is a connection between the intrinsic qualities of chosen materials and the performance of their assemblage, establishing a self-similar fractal link between the microscopic scale of materials and the building scale. What is at stake is an understanding of tectonics that transcends structural performance and embraces thermodynamics, introducing a new set of scales.

Similarly, architecture has a territorial dimension that transcends the material object to embrace the ecological geographies with which it is interconnected. This gives a territorial dimension to architecture that links building systems to the natural and artificial sources from which their material components are obtained. Material choice activates a territorial *material ecology* that breaks down the object-based understanding architectural culture has ascribed to buildings until now.

Architecture should not only be synchronized with biogeological cycles but also with the times and rhythms of briefs and users. This question, which is central nowadays, is not only connected to a laissez-faire economy that requires mutating interiors, but more importantly to the durability of buildings and their capacity to adapt to changing requirements over time. *Material infrastructures* are connected to both the paradigms of flexibility and resilience. While flexibility adapts to change through mutability, seeking out spaces that expand and contract in time, resilient buildings adapt to change through stability, defining stable spaces that can house different programmes.

The ever-increasing technological sophistication underlying building culture is, however, balanced by a renewed interest in primitivist low-cost technologies, adopting age-old construction techniques to generate passive, environmentally-aware buildings. This approach shows the potential of basic structures and materials—such as rammed earth, natural stone, wooden constructions and ceramic structures—to offer a renewed performance. A new-old building technology which, overlaying traditional monomaterial systems with a technical approach, is superseding the sophisticated technologies of active buildings with simpler passive buildings. This new trend, which blends the local and artisanal with the global and technological, is consistent with an architecture technology approach which unveils an underlying *material ethics*.

Last and not least, architecture's material culture manifests a growing concern for the human body, which is becoming one of the core questions in architecture. This interest in the human body was initially incorporated into architecture through the fields of public health and comfort. However, this emphasis on physiology began in the 1960s to be complemented by the growing interest in perception, which, transcending architecture's visual predominance, introduced a phenomenological search for holistic multisensory aesthetic experience. *Material bodies* focus on this interest in the human body, showing how material culture and environmental technologies have the capacity to generate atmospheres that have a clear influence on the perception and well-being of users inside a building.

Note:
This article is the result of combining the material reflections developed by Javier García-Germán in his PhD dissertation ("Thermodynamic Environments", ETSAM 2014) with the technological knowledge of Miquel Rodríguez (as director of xmade, building material & envelope specialists), resulting in a cross-section of the potential of contemporary architecture's materiality. In an initial common production phase, five material realms were selected, as well as paradigmatic examples of these five categories. In a later phase of coordinated production, Miquel Rodríguez curated the references and graphic material and Javier García-Germán wrote the essay.

Fig. 1a

Fig. 1b

Fig. 1c

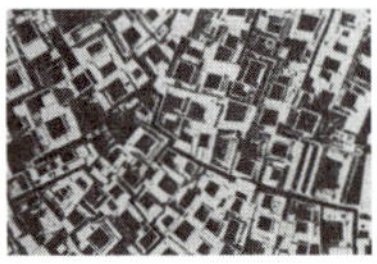
Fig. 1d

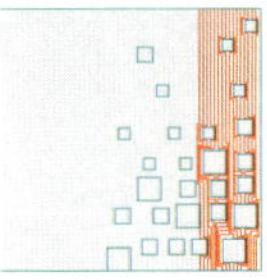
Fig. 1e

Fig. 1f

Fig. 1g

Fig. 1h

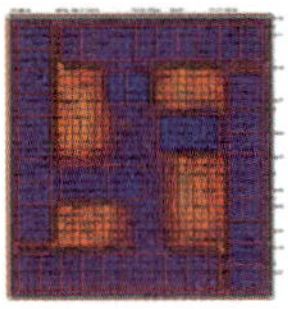
Fig. 1i

Any building, as a material construct, interacts with the local climate to create a particular microclimate inside and around a building. This spontaneous interaction generates a variety of atmospheres that vary in temperature, humidity or luminosity according to the spatial and material lineaments of the building.

These climatic interactions occur spontaneously but can also be intentionally designed. The flows of dissipating energy can be designed to achieve specific atmospheric effects. For instance, heat flows need to be harnessed, stored and dissipated when desired, and the materiality and spatial arrangement of the building plays an essential role in the design of heat flow patterns in its interior throughout the day.

From the most primitive North African climatic typologies to the technologically-enhanced radiant concrete walls of SANAA's Zollverein School of Management, or the programmatic arrangement of Baukunst + Bruther's Life Science building in Lausanne, the spatial and material arrangement of these buildings has been organized to dissipate energy in a given way. Architectural parameters—space, matter, environmental technology and programme—have been precisely orchestrated to generate specific climatic conditions.

Baukunst + Bruther's Life Science building does not only rely on specific thermodynamic devices, like the glazed gallery that envelopes the building. Its onion-ring concentric arrangement—the labs are located in the centre, the lecture rooms in the next ring and the glazed gallery in the outer ring—conflates programme and space in a convergent strategy that overlaps architectural and thermodynamic questions.

Life Science building UNIL-EPFL campus, 2020, Baukunst + Bruther.

Figs. 1a & 1b
Maison Latapie, Floirac, 1993, Lacaton & Vassal.

Figs. 1c & 1d
"Architecture without Architects", 1964, Bernard Rudofsky.

Fig. 1e
Elevation of active insulated walls, School of Management and Design, Zollverein, 2003, Transsolar.

Fig. 1f
School of Management and Design, Zollverein, 2006, Sanaa.

Fig. 1g
Haus Rauch, Schlins, 2008, Roger Boltshauser + Martin Rauch.

Figs. 1h & 1i
ICTA-ICP research centre, UAB, Cerdanyola del Vallès, H Arquitectes + DATAAE.

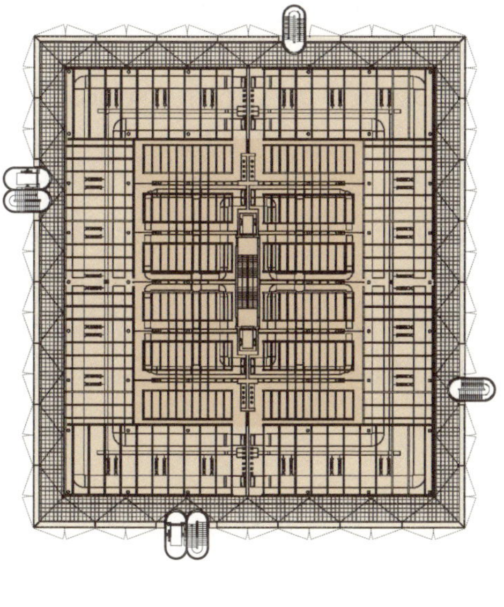

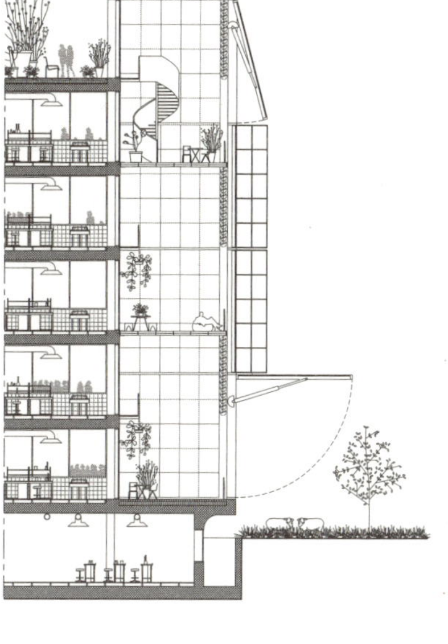

Fig. 2a

Fig. 2b

Fig. 2c

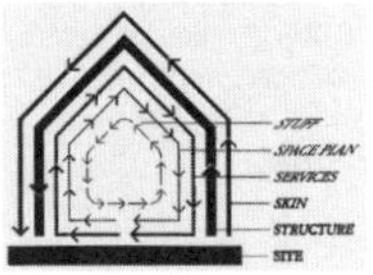

Fig. 2d

Fig. 2e

Fig. 2f

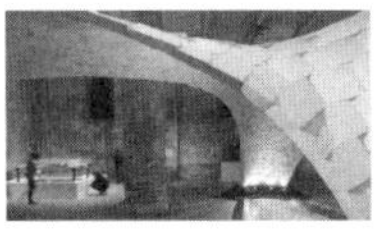
Fig. 2g

Natural ecosystems work according to laws that cycle material flows following a closed process, where outputs become raw matter for the next material input. Attuning building processes to natural dynamics requires using organic building materials, which form a part of geo-ecological spatiotemporal cycles. The current interest in wood or earth as building materials responds to this demand to synchronize building cycles with natural cycles. The work developed by the ETH Zurich Block Research Group is noteworthy, as it explores the use of wood, stone and other non-processed materials in different structural typologies. This logic also underlies the emergence of biotech building materials—such as the organic bricks produced by Ecovative, biologically cemented through fungal growth—that are grown biologically from organic materials.

Human ecologies need to replicate non-human closed loops. The need for closed industrial loops should not limit building materials to natural or organic biodegradable materials. Synthetic materials can also be used as long as they can be reintroduced in industrial cycles. This idea is at the core of Rotor, a cooperative design practice located in Brussels that investigates the organization of the material environment and has created Rotor Deconstruction, a spin-off focused on the deconstruction and reuse of building components.

The deconstruction and reuse of building systems also requires us to decouple building systems and to arrange them in independent layers according to their life cycles. This idea is crucial as it serves to assemble and disassemble building systems independently from each other and reintroduce them in urban mining dynamics.

Shigeru Ban's Tamedia AG office building in Zurich proposes a structural frame which is paradigmatic of closed material flow cycles. The fact that the building has a prefabricated timber frame using 2,000 m^3 of CNC precision-milled spruce wood is reinforced by its primitive assemblage process which, instead of using screws, nails or steel connectors, makes use of special dowels made of beech plywood for ease of disassembly, eventually enabling the reintroduction of its components into urban mining processes.

Fig. 2a
ETH Zurich Pavilion, NYC, 2015, Block Research Group.

Fig. 2b
BBConstrumat, communal areas, Barcelona, 2019, Josep Ferrando Architecture.

Fig. 2c
Swiss Sound Pavilion, Hannover, 2000, Peter Zumthor.

Fig. 2d
How Buildings Learn: What Happens After They're Built, 1994, Steward Brand.

Fig. 2e
True Talker Pavilion, Amsterdam, 2016, Studioninedots.

Fig. 2f
Plateforme réemploi, Brussels, 2019, Rotor.

Fig. 2g
Armadillo vault, Venice Biennale, 2016, Block Research Group.

Tamedia building, 2013, Shigeru Ban.

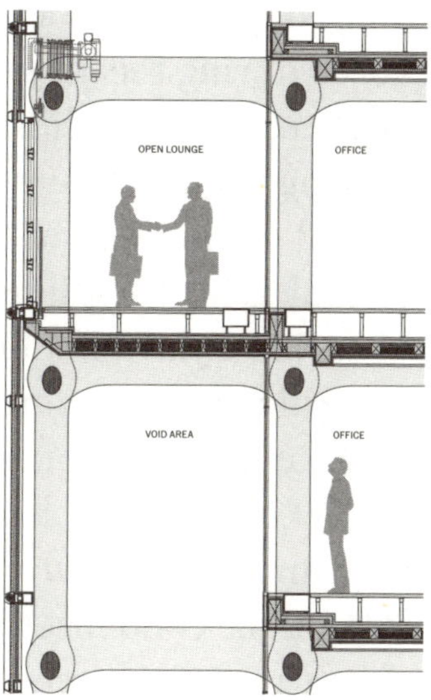

Fig. 3a

Fig. 3b

Fig. 3c

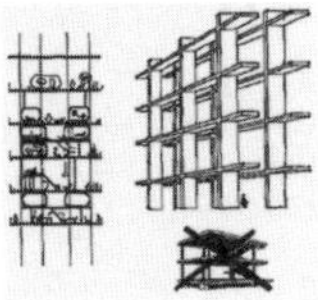
Fig. 3d

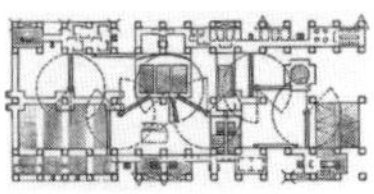
Fig. 3e

Fig. 3f

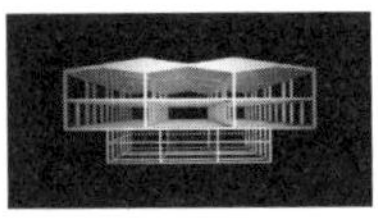
Fig. 3g

The open-building paradigm developed by John Habraken in the 1960s shed light on the contemporary need for durable and robust buildings that adapt to changing requirements over time. Habraken's work rationalized the mutating architecture proposed by Cedric Price or Archigram in paradigmatic projects such as the Fun Palace (1961) or Plug-in City (1964), proposing a clear agenda for adapting the inherent stability of buildings to changing demands. The dialectics of support versus infill allowed for a sequenced spatial strategy compatible with mainstream building arrangements, enabling architecture to be managed over time. These ideas are still present, and an array of recent buildings, such as NEXT21 in Osaka and NEST (Next Evolution in Sustainable Building Technologies) in Dübendorf, research building technologies that enable the dichotomy between support and infill.

However, the interest in buildings as open infrastructures is not limited to the dialectics between stable structures and exchangeable components. This idea was presented decades ago by Herman Hertzberger, who pointed out the capacity of historical buildings—such as Venetian palazzos or Jaisalmer's havelis—to adapt to changing uses through the neutral geometry of their rooms' stability.

This question is present in the contemporary search for architectural layouts which, in their indeterminacy, have the capacity to house a variety of uses. The interest in a simple and neutral architecture is connected to its capacity to articulate generic spaces that will have the capacity to adapt to unanticipated future uses. The work of practices such as Lacaton & Vassal, OFFICE and MUOTO has explored during recent years the capacity of uniform generic spatial grids to produce a non-specific and undetermined architecture that can adapt to changing requirements.

Is there a specific materiality and technology of open buildings? Is there an infrastructural tectonics that attunes building processes with changing uses? Steward Brandt's shearing layers offer an interesting strategy that overlays building layers according to their durability, introducing an unfinished aesthetic which is at the core of this question.

Practices such as French MUOTO opt for simple and durable building strategies that are coherent with an *infrastructural materiality* that is more necessary than ever. MUOTO's public condenser in Paris Saclay underlines the need for durable architectural strategies. This building has been conceived as a minimal structure, using rough materials, robust and long-lasting techniques, deploying very simple building technologies that are lasting and do not require complicated maintenance, highlighting the material tectonics open buildings need.

Fig. 3a
EMPA Nest building, Zurich, 2016, Gramazio Kohler, Ing. Joseph Schwartz.

Fig. 3b
Takara Beautilion, Osaka, 1970, Kisho Kurokawa.

Fig. 3c
Smart Living Lab, Fribourg, 2019, Behnisch + Partner.

Fig. 3d
Open building, 1961, John Habraken.

Fig. 3e
Fun Palace, London, 1965, Cedric Price.

Fig. 3f
School of architecture, Nantes, 2009, Lacaton & Vassal.

Fig. 3g
Hofacker school building, Zurich, 2020, E2A.

Public condenser, 2016, MUOTO.

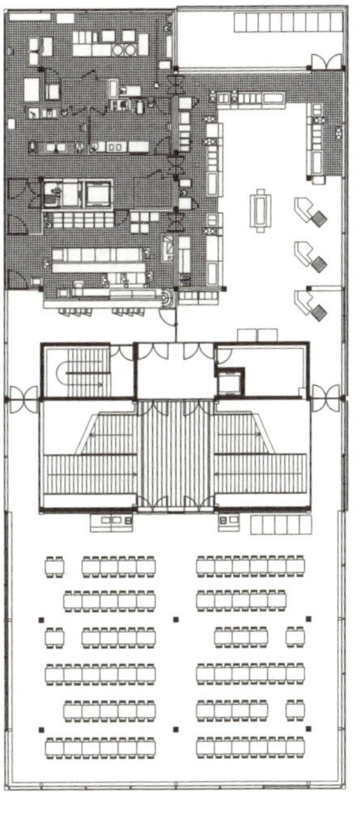

Fig. 4a

Contemporary tectonics display contradictory tendencies. The ever-increasing technological sophistication of industrial prefabricated building processes and energy-efficient eco-tech buildings is currently balanced by a renewed interest in primitivist low-cost technologies.

Fig. 4b

The material strategies used by practices such as TED'A Architects, Anna Heringer and Francis Kéré employ building techniques such as load-bearing rammed-earth walls or brick masonry, thereby boosting local and artisanal practices. The building procedures they use are in keeping with the appropriate technology movement, deploying a technological apparatus in keeping with its economic and social context.

Fig. 4c

Fig. 4d

Fig. 4e

Fig. 4f

Fig. 4g

Heringer's work is paradigmatic of these practices, which deploy a counter-globalization agenda. The DESI Training Center in Rudrapur (2010) is a vocational school for electrical training in a rural area in Bangladesh. It is built with the traditional rammed-earth and bamboo techniques which are typical of this region. However, they have been upgraded with Western technology to improve their resistance to humidity. The building's foundations are rendered with cement plaster, and a double sheet of locally available polyethylene waterproofs the roof, making the building last longer and reducing maintenance requirements. This project is a clear example of an architectural practice that aims to communicate and develop knowledge and skills within the local population so that they can make the best possible use of their available resources. Historic building techniques are developed and improved, and the skills passed on to local tradesmen.

Nonetheless, these nostalgia-driven regional positions, even though they are very necessary in their regional contexts, cannot be widely used, as they are not applicable to massive housing developments in urban agglomerations. They need to be addressed by an optimistic approach that combines age-old techniques with industrial procedures to produce a cosmopolitan and multicultural *material ethic.*

Brandlhuber's Antivilla in Potsdam deploys an architectural strategy that departs from sophisticated star-system tectonics to show the material crudeness of building processes. In this transformation of an existing warehouse into a suburban house, the original building elements are upgraded with very simple architectural interventions that transform this banal industrial architecture with a coarse but optimistic ethical domesticity, bringing a cosmopolitan perspective to traditional building procedures.

Fig. 4a
Chai Viticole, Vauvert, 1998, Gilles Perraudin.

Fig. 4b
Can Jordi i n'Àfrica, Montuïri, Mallorca, 2016, TEd'A arquitectes.

Fig. 4c
Primary school, Gando, 2001, Kéré architecture.

Fig. 4d
Meti school, Rudrapur, 2005, Anna Heringer + Eike Roswag.

Fig. 4e
Tanzhaus, Zurich, 2020, Barozzi/Veiga.

Fig. 4f
Haus Rauch, Schlins, 2008, Roger Boltshauser (spec. Martin Rauch).

Fig. 4g
Ricola storage building, Laufen, 2014, Herzog & de Meuron (spec. Martin Rauch).

Antivilla, 2014, Brandlhuber + Emde, Burlon.

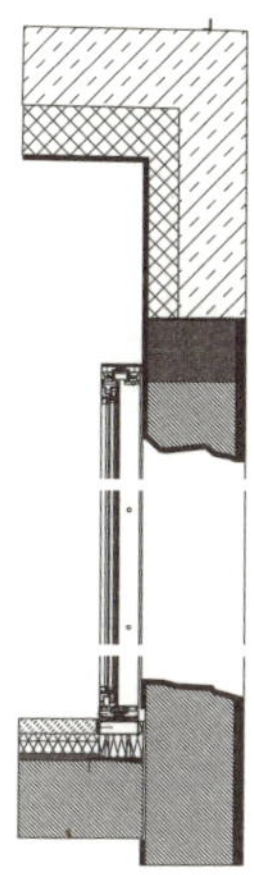

Fig. 5a

Fig. 5b

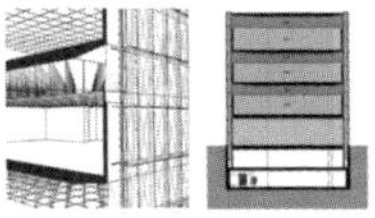

Fig. 5c

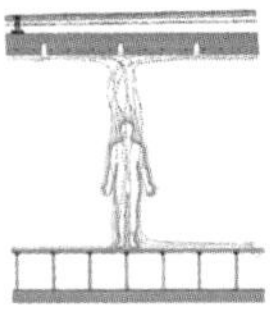

Fig. 5d

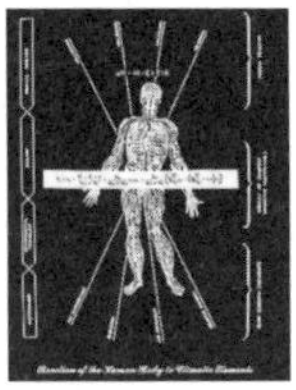

Fig. 5e

Fig. 5f

Fig. 5g

Even though the human body was incorporated into architecture through the fields of public health and hygiene, and later through the paradigm of comfort, this initial focus on physiology was decades later complemented by an interest in psychology that introduced a sensorial dimension, combining body and mind.

Recent studies are questioning Freud's strict separation of body and mind, revealing the fact that the psychological reactions of the body are connected to the physiological, creating a continuity of environment, soma and human perception. These advances will, in the not too distant future, serve to design environments with precise knowledge of the reactions that atmospheric effects bring about in the human body.

The design of atmospheres has been principally explored during recent years through art installations and expo pavilions. It is important to point out the work developed by artist Olafur Eliasson who, in well-known installations such as *Beauty* (1993) or *The Weather Project* (Tate Modern 2003), showed the capacity of atmosphere to induce a specific aesthetic sensorial experience.

Within the field of architecture, Philippe Rahm has developed a series of installations, such as *Hormonorium* for the Swiss Pavilion at the Venice Biennale 2002, in which he critically explores the connections between atmosphere and the human body, underlining the importance of non-visible phenomena in architectural experience.

Terrain's Austrian Pavilion for the Milan Expo 2015, though still part of this series of architectural and artistic experiments, can be considered one of the first examples of the atmospheric being generated by means of built elements—in this case, the interaction between a body of plants and trees, and a temporary construction that forms a patio—instead of using special effects. The proposal introduced a fragment of a European forest into the Expo. This biological graft attempted not only to show visitors the Austrian landscape, but also to demonstrate the lower temperatures induced by this patch of European forest, overlapping exhibition programme, human well-being and sensorial experience.

Fig. 5a
Blur building, Swiss Expo, Yverdon-les-Bains, 2002, Diller Scofidio + Renfro.

Fig. 5b
Fog Assembly, Palais de Versailles, 2016, Olafur Eliasson.

Figs. 5c & 5d
Thermally Active Surfaces in Architecture, 2010, Kiel Moe.

Fig. 5e
Design with Climate, 1963, Victor + Aladar Olgyay.

Fig. 5f
Porch building, CONCYTEC office competition, Lima, 2015, Javier García-Germán + TAAs.

Fig. 5g
"Hormonorium", Swiss Pavilion, Venice Biennale, 2002, Décosterd & Rahm.

Austrian Pavilion, Milan Expo, 2015, Klaus Loenhart (Terrain).

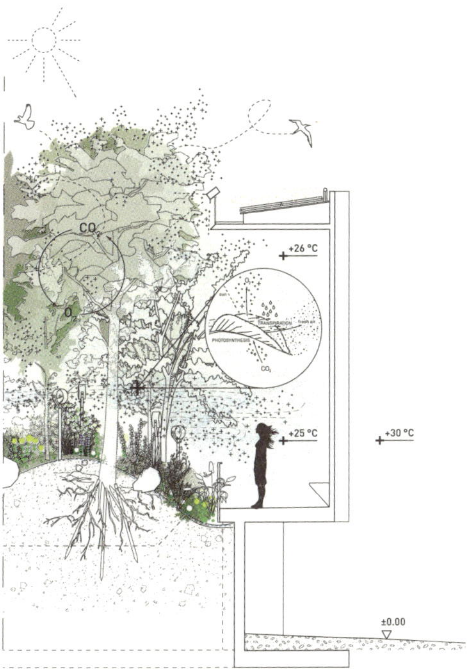

David Bestué

Three-Dimensional Poems

98

In autumn 2017, I presented the *ROSI AMOR* exhibition at the Reina Sofia National Museum in Madrid. In one of the rooms I wanted to draw relationships between the poetic act and sculpture through a series of three-dimensional poems. I wanted to relate my practice to poetry because I am interested in how it suspends language by creating its own grammar rules. Somehow, sculpture also suspends the object: being stripped of use it also resists a single meaning. That is why I wanted to investigate the possible transformation of a series of texts into sculptures. To make this possible, I used three references: the Nativity façade of the Sagrada Familia in Barcelona, a pâté, and the poet César Vallejo.

When designing the sculptural whole of the Nativity façade of the Sagrada Familia, Antoni Gaudí wanted to represent a giant nativity scene with examples of the mineral, vegetable and animal kingdoms. The architect wanted to present God's work in the façade, and to this end he decided to make moulds of those elements that he wanted to appear in the façade, such as palms, geese and people. In several images from his workshop that have been preserved, a multitude of plaster positives are seen that later were transformed into stone by means of carving by pointing machine. So he rejected the mediation of representation that the expertise of the sculptors would have offered him, in favour of a literal copy of reality. It was this example that prompted my interest in the use of moulds. For me, they are the zero degree of representation, a transfer process in which the shape of the copied element is permanently recorded. An inorganic element that is a formal memory of an organic element or a gesture that has already disappeared. However, although I liked this method, I found the range of materials used to make positives very limited. And that was when the paté appeared.

At Christmas in Barcelona, special little cold meats are marketed: they have figurative silhouettes and they are filled with nuts and olives. One of the ones I like most is a duck-shaped paté. Apparently it is nothing special but from the point of view of sculpture it is unique due to the agreement between form and material. Actually, it is somewhat perverse to think that this food product is the representation of an animal made with a fragment of that same animal. When I saw that reverberation between form and material, I realized that I could work the matter in a similar way to how poets choose words. Just as they select and tidy up a series of concepts, I could do the same with a set of materials. Matter is the hinge between the mental and the physical, between word and form. There are sculptures that, by their form, can refer to many different things, notions that are outside them, but the material is what relates them to the real, what constitutes them. That is why matter is above shape and the construction and destruction of an object. Matter is always present; when history has gone, when the original meaning of the sculpture is no longer known, the matter remains; it is its anchor in the here and now.

I would like to show the common points of these two examples that I just explained: on the one hand, we have a plaster work that is the product of a mould and, on the other, a work whose shape is somewhat childish but made of the material it represents. We could join the two techniques to make a mould and fill it with the material of the moulded object, but in this case we would obtain a copy of the object itself. For that reason, I deboned the relationship between matter and form, separating it, and to do so I let myself be guided by the work of César Vallejo.

César Vallejo is a Peruvian poet who related to language in an almost chemical way, joining and mixing words and inventing neologisms. For example, *Trilce* is the name of one of his great poems, and is the result of mixing two words: *triste* (sad) and *dulce* (sweet). The creation of this type of words, in which their outlines are cracked open and they merge with each other, was similar to the way in which I was filling moulds of different objects with materials of different origins. To make the moulds I chose a series of objects and furniture from Carabanchel, the neighbourhood where I had my studio at that time. I wanted my sculptures to look like domestic items at first sight, like the ones stacked in thrift shops. After making the negatives in silicone, which were like empty bowls, I filled them with powdered materials mixed with resin, which acted as a binder.

I wanted the materials to revolve around the emotional substrate of the country, using their poetic production as a sieve. To this end, I took as my basis a series of places and imaginations extracted from Spanish poetry, present in the work of writers such as Luis de Góngora and Aníbal Nuñez, or Juan Ramón Jiménez and María Zambrano. One of the things that interested me about these materials was that they were from precise places. In the same way that many poets described landscapes, rivers or specific trees, I wanted to do the same with my selection, choosing components from multiple sources: an old elm to which Antonio Machado dedicated a poem in Soria or a ravine called Clamores to which María Zambrano dedicated an article. In this way I gave my sculptures a kind of twofold presence: on the one hand, the place of their material origin and, on the other, the one occupied by the same work in the exhibition space. Beaches, mountains and cathedrals were undone, crushed, deformed, liquefied and pulverized. They stopped being to become something else. By grinding these elements, I atomized their substance so that they could acquire a new body just after disappearing; I diluted the visible to put everything on the same level. In the process, they were reminiscent of natural dissolutions such as sand, dust, gravel, ash or flour.

The works shown below are the result of this process that were exhibited in the museum. However, when I was finishing production I realized that there was a fundamental problem in what I had done. In an interview with Jaime Gil de Biedma by Federico Campbell, the poet commented that, for him, the real thing was not a mountain or a tree but what was happening between them—that is, conflicts, injustices or desire. How could I pulverize that? I couldn't. There are concepts that are not physical and that move around among what is: fleeting events, spoken words, modes or thoughts. When I wanted to make three-dimensional poems, I noticed that the poem is not only a material fact; it also a force field, with its links and relationships (syntax). This certainty clashes with the limitations of the sculptural format, though there will certainly be a way to accommodate, somehow, those invisible powers.

Valdemingómez slag wheel. Epic and lyric (plate of ruin and garden). Transition from meat to wood. Building (floor hung from pillar hung from roof). Apple of 9/11 ashes on stool with particles of the Berlin Wall. Salt shelving with Atocha jam on Cerro Testigo plate. Cypress bucket with pathway handle.

A and B (fragment of place where a person was born and fragment of place where that same person died). Brain hanger and saliva wire. Rose, orange blossom and honeysuckle lamp. Vegetable table traversed by Cuelgamuros with sweet slice of bitter melon. Coffee, milk and sugar grille. Seawater table on four fish legs with Moguer sock and boat branch. Key of Ur on stepladder with mineral, vegetable and animal step and pieces of five continents in the base. Broken ravine glass. Old elm candle on bone brick.

Flour table with gesso bread and bridge bone. Palm-tree slat with nail of tooth and lip of carnation. Bar and ring (furnishing and vase). Banana stool with garlic back and Delphi garlic. Toledo Cathedral bottle on a stool of wine. Trestles and table top of Monegros earth with Ebro riverbed base, concave fossil, two olive bullets and sergeant of swamp, castle and hill holding a circular smoke mat. Blue angle, skin angle, blue angle and desert angle on tomato rug. Roman pottery cup and Numantia flower on industrial estate boards with butterfly hinge. Blood motor on sand bench and bone and marble cups.

Taking advantage of the revelations offered by reading a construction detail, this section pairs up two constructions of a domestic nature, Villa Hammer and Mas JEC. The two share similar considerations and conditions that ultimately materialize in very different and personal ways. In both cases, the project integrates a pre-existing condition that is transformed and expanded, giving the whole a new architectural meaning. The two houses incorporate contemporary cosmetic techniques that set architecture in its time, meanwhile freeing it from stylistic dogmatisms, linguistically defining independent architectures. The floor plans of Villa Hammer and Mas JEC have disobedient and misaligned geometries, with cosy corners and unexpected dimensions that are perceived and understood only by the experience of inhabiting. Behind their domesticity these two projects conceal clear decisions that demonstrate the presence of a very near technical and environmental future, and a consistent memory integrated in the present.

Herzog & de Meuron & Sauter von Moos
VILLA HAMMER, Basel, 2014–2018

Built by Heinrich Flügel in 1895, Villa Hammer is a stately neo-baroque villa in the Kleinbasel neighbourhood next to the Wettstein-Square. Despite being listed, the building was completely rundown after its last owner died and victim to a series of poorly executed renovations that destroyed large parts of the original interiors. Following the client's commission, the old villa was gently renovated and complemented by a newly constructed building in the rear. Two architectural offices—a team from Herzog & de Meuron and the architecture duo Sauter von Moos—at different times provided their specific contributions to the project, as they were responsible for both its design and execution.

Renovation of the old house involves reappropriating its initial spatial layout around an inner hall with a light-flooded stairwell, climatically improving the entire structure and adapting it to its new use as a day-care centre. The architects also rejuvenated its exterior appearance, inserting in the garden—a wildly growing biotope and car park—a new building containing two apartments.

Adding density to the urban location, the new addition encompasses the maximum space obtainable according to present building regulations. The elongated ground floor, continuing the existing one-storey annexe of the villa, delimits the site towards the east. It embraces a protected garden that is reached via a newly produced neo-post-baroque portal which, together with a formally similar open shelter, frames the entrance court. A two-storey cubic volume covered by a wide overhanging roof is placed at the centre of the rear building's extension. Its façades are penetrated by tall vertical openings that unify the volume and relate it to the scale and formal language of the existing villa.

The ground floor apartment receives through its open front façade as much daylight as possible. The large kitchen, which one immediately enters through the foyer, structures it internally. Above, the upper apartment is more enclosed within massive walls that contain precise openings to view the beautiful surroundings, yet opens on its northern and southern sides towards two generous terraces. Inside, the pronouncement of the longitudinal and vertical axes seeks to add a sense of greater space to the rather small-scale rooms.

The ensemble of the new building and the villa stands in a critical dialogue—the new structure emulates the old, but also demarcates its own contemporaneity: what was formerly done in heavy stone, is now done in lighter wood and steel; what appears to obey the tenets of a classic centralized order is resting on a dematerialized plinth; what generally follows a strict formal canon permits the accommodation of informal pragmatic distortions; and, as is most tangible in the large ornaments engulfing the windows but also in the newly added ancillary structures, what was once carved out by stonemasons is now brought to fresh expression using digital technologies.

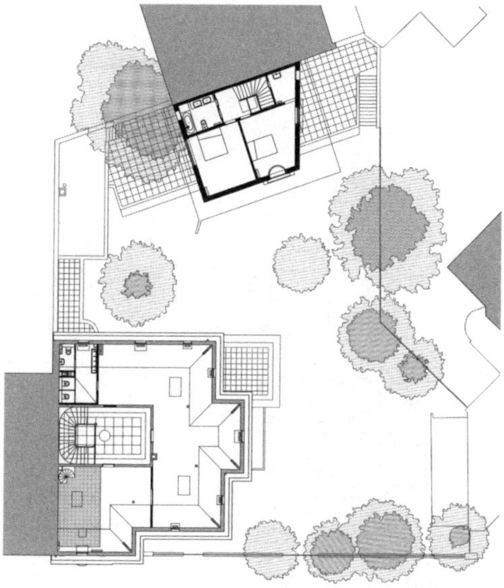

Second floor

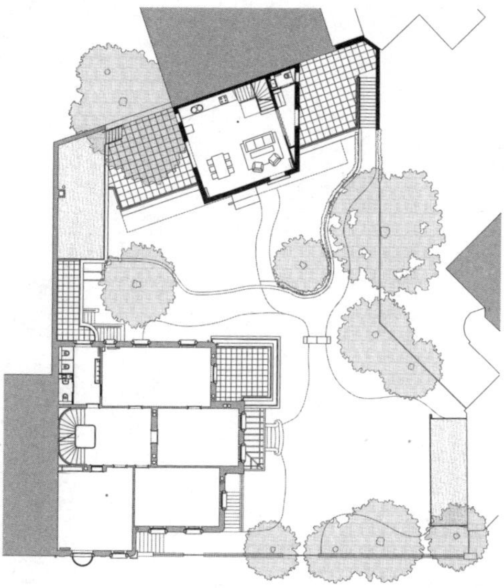

First floor

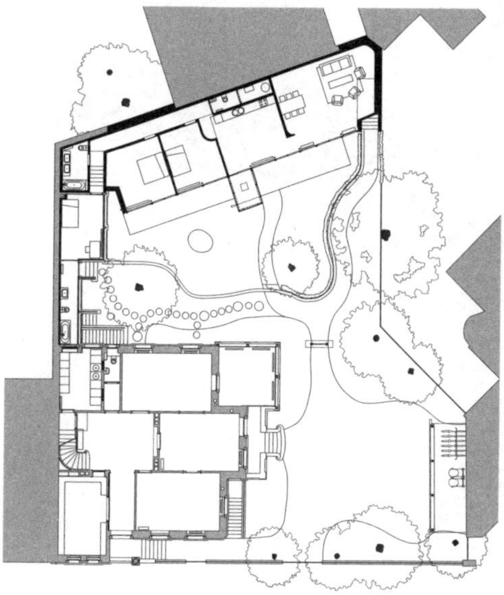

Ground floor

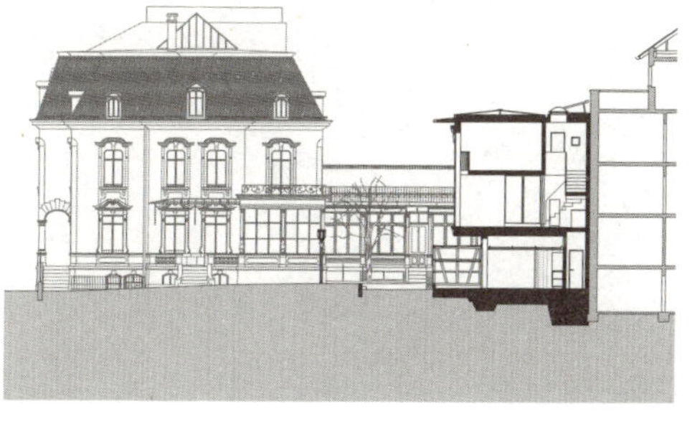

We supplemented the protected Villa Hammer with a new building in order to create additional living space. It is not merely a renovation: the villa was analysed in its urban context and developed further. Hence, the addition must convince both with regard to town planning and in its interaction with the historical substance—but simultaneously should also be perceived as a distinct piece of architecture from the twenty-first century.

Pierre de Meuron

Aixopluc
MAS JEC, Reus, 2017–2018

This habitat's genealogy starts in 1932, when the Casas family built a fifty square-metre one-floor *maset* in the rural outskirts of Reus. The place had housed four different families, survived fascist attacks during the Civil War, and had grown one floor up, becoming a *mas* with an orchard, a big palm tree, and some large shade trees, when JEC's late parents bought it in 1975. After several years of additions and transformations, including a cellar and a garage, they moved in with their son in 1982. The father, using his skills as a watchmaker, spent his free time patiently assembling, welding, screwing and adding all kinds of rooms, huts, shacks, sheds, porches and shade structures, using offcuts, leftover pieces of metal, clock mechanisms and rather loose techniques that freed him from the precision needed in his day job. He carefully built an outdoors abode, a second open house around the original *mas*. The site was in a perpetual state of construction. And then, in 2015, the father died, and the place stood empty. A year after the father's passing, the son, his wife and daughter—JEC—decided to move back in. They contacted us with just one question: whether it was better to keep the *mas*, or to demolish it and build a brand-new structure instead.

What made this place inhabitable? Its value was not the existing main house. Although its heterogeneous structure was in quite good shape, what made it extraordinary were its self-built garden structures and trees. These shelters represent the real quality of this site. There was no way we could design them. They were unlikely to be reproduced. They were extremely fragile, to the point that it seemed impossible to repair them. They were highly complex, with no separation between structure and envelope. They were unregulated. Some of them had asbestos roofs. Designed without a plan, following no building code. Nothing superfluous or extremely necessary, everything an invention. As architects, tied by legal and safety constraints, stuck with design tools full of distance, hands impoverished, this posed an enormous and humbling challenge. How not to devastate these ways of life and this affection? Could we make up a reality where our fictions by design engaged with these other, unattainable fictions? How could we respect and nourish the built love we found there?

We did not keep the old *mas* as it was, nor did we totally demolish it. Instead, we added more inhabitable air, in the worst area of the plot. The extension is related to the existing porches. We kept its weight light, like a porch, using CLT panels, thin steel tubes and cork. By maintaining the old construction, we created a small compound that the family will use according to their changing needs through the seasons and decades. We erased any trace of brief or specific use inside the old *mas*. Kitchen, gone. Bathrooms, gone. Bedrooms, gone. First floor, half gone. A space devoid of any programmatic constraint, just an interior with high thermal inertia and a Norwegian fireplace.

Now, we needed to take the asbestos away. Some porches had to be disassembled to access and repair the façades. In order to grant us the building permit, the local authorities asked us to dismantle two of the existing unregulated roofs. This was an opportunity to increase the diversity of the outdoor places. One of these rooms became a patio. In another, the asbestos and plastic sheets were replaced by cables that will guide vines for new leafy roofs. We took out more than we added. Wrinkles and cracks were cleaned up. Some we had to cover with mortar. Others we just painted. A modest skin treatment, more rouge than botox. Slightly greasy hair combed down with cheap cologne when a hot shower was not to be had. This house exudes the Royale Ambrees and Varon Dandys of the family and friends who built it, not the Dior or organic perfumes of the people reading this. A final coincidence brought in a builder who was family to JEC. He had some masons with whom we developed ad hoc masonry units, quite different from the ones we had designed in our BIM digital model.

The son grew up contemplating his father's patient constructions and eating Sunday *paellas* in a roofless kitchen. He learnt to trust and respect people who built for their family. To understand the fertile embrace of imprecision and love, the unprejudiced acceptance of error and immediate craft as an opportunity. He passed this trust to us, and it was a blessing. We had to give up the search for perfection and listen. Only by talking to the dead do they become ancestors and not ghosts. A legacy to dwell within, not a reality or a fiction.

Note: JEC is an acronym of the three inhabitants' names, but it also means winter coat in Catalan.

Ground floor

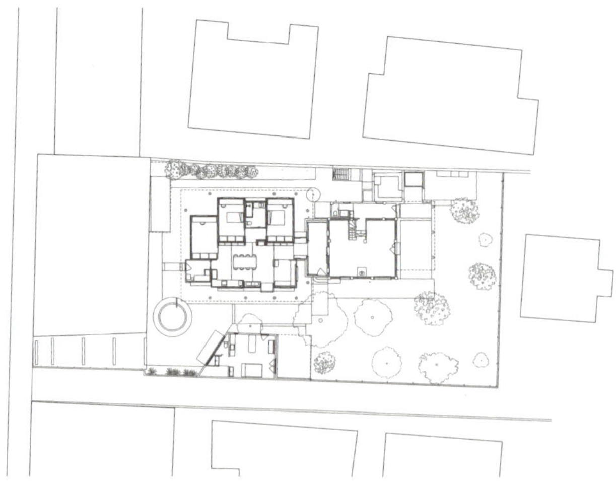

First floor

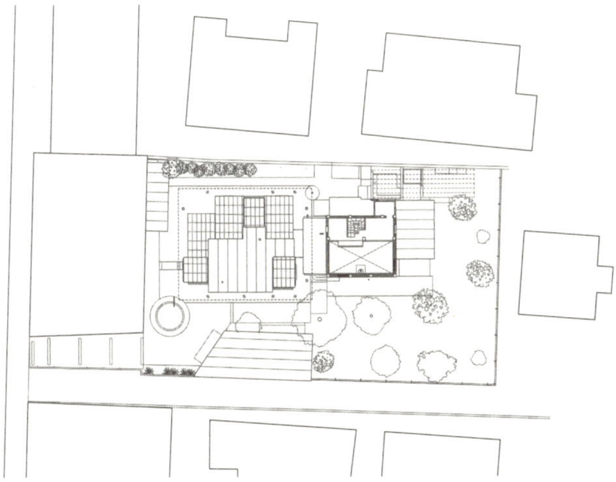

Roof floor

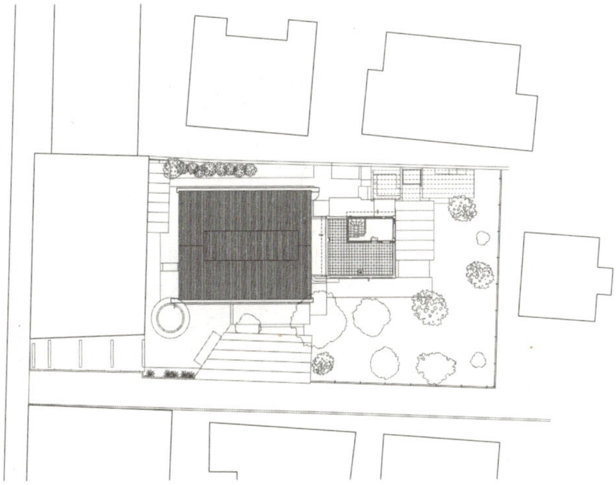

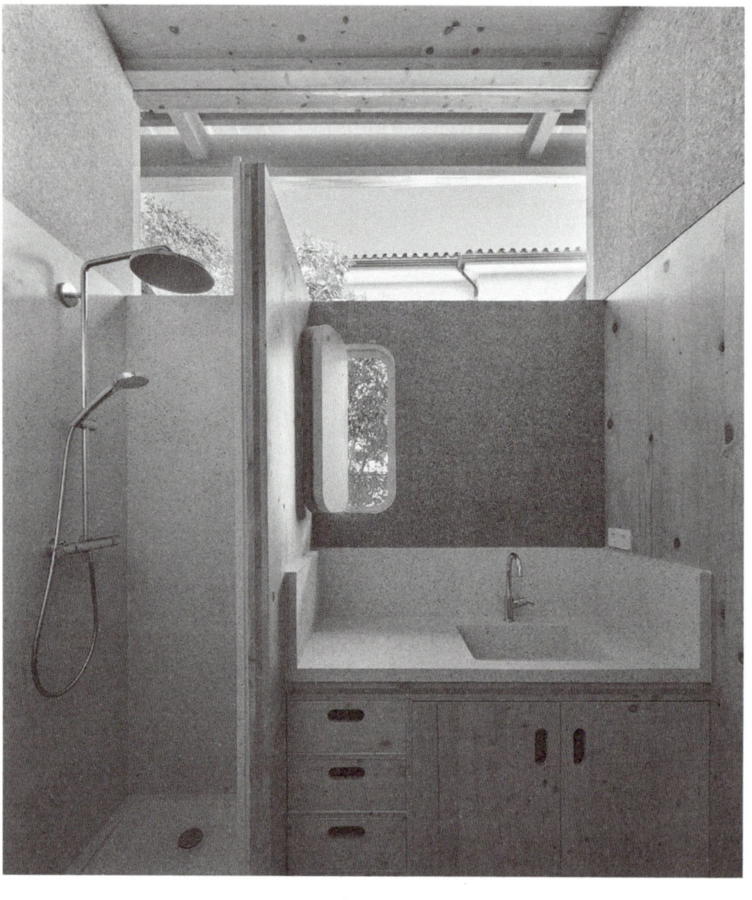

Epilogue

Interview with Addenda, Estar & Barozzi/Veiga

As an epilogue, we include a collective interview with three architecture studios that share the distinctive feature of operating abroad from Santiago de Compostela and Barcelona: Estar, Barozzi/Veiga and Addenda. The interview addresses three issues, and does so in relation to the content developed in each of the three sections that structures *Quaderns* 272:

> the relationship between architecture and the city (scale 1),
> the definition of the identity of an architectural object (scale 2) and
> the implementation of a structural detail (scale 3).

These three scales illustrate the development of different "cosmetic techniques"[1] and, consequently, the construction of personal awareness, and of imagined identities in a foreign context.

Each studio was asked the same three questions and requested to answer on the basis of the experience gained from the development of a single project.[2] Project documents that illustrate the reflections of the authors accompany each response.

1
The essay "The Cunning of Cosmetics" by Jeffrey Kipnis analyses the first stage of the work of Herzog & de Meuron and coined the expression "cosmetic techniques", understood as a project strategy between ornamentation and minimalism. *El Croquis*, No. 84, 1997.

2
Ancien Manège (Geneva, Switzerland), Estar (Aurora Armental and Stefano Ciurlo); Musée Cantonal des Beaux-Arts (Lausanne, Switzerland), Barozzi/Veiga (Fabrizio Barozzi and Alberto Veiga); Bauhaus Museum Dessau (Dessau, Germany), Addenda (Cecilia Rodríguez, Arnau Sastre, Anne Hinz, José Zabala and Roberto González).

The Face of the City. Scale 1

The relationship between architecture and city is considered key to the definition of a project. In this sense, it would be possible to identify three types of urban relations: establishing links between architecture and the city, proposing a desired autonomy, and opting for a certain urban indifference. The choice of each determines the nature of the architectural response.

In the European context, the relationship between architecture and city acquires special relevance when defining a transformation of an established area, and also when building a new fragment of the city, either in the centre or on the periphery. This relationship inevitably raises a debate about the importance of local cultural and social values, and the influence or incorporation of others of a more global nature.

What is the relationship between your building and the city and how do you think it participates in the construction of contemporary urban settings in the European context?

A.

The building of the Bauhaus school in Dessau remains the epicenter of activity and movement of visitors in the town. In recent years, and especially in 2019 (the centenary of the Bauhaus), this role has only increased

the draw of the most representative historical buildings (school, teachers' houses—Meisterhäuser—, etc.). But the town centre has not benefited by this activity since these buildings are located in the northwest of the town, segregated by the railroad track.

Therefore, the choice of the location of the new museum responds fundamentally to a political decision: to insert an activity mechanism (in this case a cultural amenity for exhibitions and different types of events promoted by the Bauhaus Dessau Foundation) with the intention of generating a cultural hub of attraction and gathering in the central park area (Stadtpark) of Dessau, near the town hall and the historic centre.

The placing of the museum in the park—up to now a public and completely open space—was not without criticism. Even more so when the characteristics of the objects in the Bauhaus archive to be exhibited required a hermetic space protected from the outside. The shape and position of the building are a direct and simple response to the requirements outlined to activate the place: a glass box (a changing material, sensitive to environmental conditions) containing a concrete bridge-building that houses the permanent collection and frees up the maximum space on the ground floor, located in continuity with the street that connects the old area with the town park.

But not only were the social and site conditions essential in defining the architecture of the building—so was the economy of the project. Initially, the interior bridge-structure was metallic and clad in wood. The budgetary restrictions meant that, in the end, this structure was fully executed in bare concrete. We consider this circumstance to be a success from the contextual point of view, since the park is currently surrounded by buildings from the GDR era, built of prefabricated concrete elements (Plattenbau). Therefore, the architecture of the building is also a response to the condition of the current economic precariousness and what we call "The Age of Less" (after the Miesian "Less is more").

E.

The Ancien Manège was built between 1828 and 1829 to house the military riding arena in the historic centre of Geneva. Its volumetric composition by parts follows the architectural canons of the early nineteenth century: a large covered central arena, two lower volumes to the sides for the stables, a semi-circular *rotonda* as an entrance, and four towers defining the corners of the building.

In 1930, with the substitution of the horse by motor vehicles, the building was transformed into a service station and garage. In 1950, to be used as a carpark, the Manège was considerably transformed; two large floor slabs in the central space and ramps in one of the side volumes were built with site-mixed concrete. The building was used in this configuration for vehicle parking until 2018.

One of the urban scenarios that the project of the Ancien Manège proposes is of a social and collective nature. As it was an under-utilized resource and inaccessible to the public, a participatory process began, promoted by local residents the historical centre, who formed an association to find ways to restore the building to the city. It was the beginning of a long process that led to a public competition organized by the Geneva municipality that we won in late 2014.

From a formal point of view, our proposal seeks to re-establish the volumetric essence of the building. To achieve this, the project proposes the partial demolition of the extension built during the 1950s, partly eliminating one of the two floors and the ramps to the upper levels of the parking space. This operation brings natural light into the interior and serves to restore a large space in the central nave.

This demolition restores the composition of naves on each side of the central volume and introduces a terrace on the first floor, accessible from the large central hall. During the project process, the towers were redrawn, and minimal adjustments were made in the composition of façade

openings; the large doorways to the garage were glazed to create new relations between interior and street.

Because access to the Manège was originally on horseback and later by car, we had to redefine the idea of entrance and public space. Its design is based on the experience of visiting other entry ways in the historic city, but in the case of the Manège, it seeks to define a more civic character. The entrance is considered an urban space, open to the public whenever there is activity in the building. It is a key component for the return of the building to the material and social context of the historic centre of Geneva, as well as for its comprehension, given the coexistence in this space of construction elements from the nineteenth century, 1950s and later, and the fact that the ground crosses the threshold as an extension of public space.

On the other hand, the idea of belonging to the city is achieved by the design and construction of building details developed with local specialists from each trade: the treatment of natural stone, the substitution of lime mortars, lime paints, the fitting of exterior wood joinery, the redefinition of copper roof details and the choice of clay roof tiles. All these interventions are related, establishing a dialogue with the historic city, adapting to current technical and programmatic requirements, and allowing the building to be seen as a part of its material and historical context.

B/V.

Lausanne's case is quite useful for answering this question. The project clearly expresses its desire to create a city. It is inextricably linked to the city thanks to the opening of a new urban space, a large, elongated square that aims to connect the city to this new area formed by the three museums.

Our projects are always born with the will to complete the city, to be part of it. Therefore, the architectural object is always dependent on the relationship with the public. In fact, this definition of public space is always the driving impulse of any of our projects, from the first designs to the most recent.

We always understand the city as a continuous whole, we never see it as the aggregation of objects; that's why the project always starts with the desire to be part of something. This projective pattern is undoubtedly indebted to a reading of the European city in which we have grown as a studio.

In relation to this and also to answer the second part of the question, we have seen over the years how this approach has also helped us in projects in Asia and the United States, where the urban is understood and shaped in another way. Even in very heterogeneous, fragmented and

incoherent contexts, often an expression of Asian cities, we have always sought to be part of a whole. Or, at least launch elements capable of establishing links with the city.

These reflections almost always refer to how projects settle into a geography, in a territory. Subsequently we have always explained how the projects seek their own ground between the specificity of the place and a formal autonomy and how, from this relationship, from the search for this balance, the way to build a language for the project emerges.

In the text "A Sentimental Monumentality" we explain this relationship, so fundamental for us.

Surface and Depth. Scale 2

During the last decade, and especially in Europe, contemporary architecture has shown interest in the value of what has already been built, both for its historical interest and also for its environmental value. This situation has also been accompanied by greater attention to the user, rather overlooked in some important projects. This architecture, attentive to the value of the existing and the integration of the social, moves away from rather utopian positions, and leads, as a strategy, to the recreation of known, almost familiar situations, both interior and exterior.

The importance of the known during the conception of architectural identity does not, however, mean renouncing the search for the unexpectedly new and original. This process inevitably addresses the debate on subjectivity, and therefore, the meaning of architecture.

What is your thinking about the value of existing architecture? How do you manage architectural subjectivity and meaning during the definition of a project?

A.

According to Hermann Czech, "what exists is stronger than anything that one can invent in its place". And if place occupies the previous answer, to answer this second question, about what exists, something approaching the idea of Bauhaus is required. For this, we try the negative path of Meister Eckhart or Nicholas of Cusa, taking a paradoxical journey that seeks the radical denial of all the definitions of God, transcending reason without abandoning it. In this sense, we experience the theological liberation of the mystics. Within the existing we consider several areas or spectrums, some visible and tangible, such as the shape and programme of a building, and others invisible and intangible, such as economics or socio-political issues and aspirations. Sometimes the existing reality also refers to

the past, to a state that has already disappeared, destroyed or deformed, although very present in local memory. All these areas add value to the architecture, complementing and completing it. Interestingly, the name of our office has a lot to do with this issue: architecture as an addition or complement to existing reality (with the intention of modifying, correcting or improving it).

To talk about our subjective contribution we need another digression, this time based on the Adorno's approach to the atrophy of functionalism as an architectural period and the dilemma of overcoming it without going backwards. Although functionalism is arbitrary, the reasons lie not in architecture but outside. The objectivity proposed by Adorno seeks non-delegated reasons, organizing principles that come from architecture itself. This is our subjective contribution: a contribution not delegated to the agreed-upon subjectivities that build the architectural project. In some way, our projects are characterized by a certain lack of identity as a result of being generated by a process of contamination and combination of different ideas and personal notions or subjectivities. In this order of things, there is also a topic that has been very important since the competition phase, and that is the relational issue, introduced in the project working with Moritz Küng (curator and independent art and architecture editor), when we tested the functionality of the ground floor space based on the work of contemporary artists such as Dominique Gonzalez-Foerster, Richard Venlet and Félix González-Torres. For example, one reflection that we find fun (and not as crazy as it might seem initially), based on Dominique Gonzalez-Foerster's idea of tropicalization: if our building is a reinterpretation of the São Paulo Museum of Art (MASP) by Lina Bo Bardi, it is thought-provoking to think that, by relating the two buildings, we are tropicalizing Dessau, a process that could be accelerated due to climate change.

E.

Our way of working, either at the scale of a territory, a garden, a building or furniture, is always based on careful observation of what exists physically. We like to observe closely how something is structured and we try to comprehend why it is that way and how it became what it is today. We engage in this process without a preconceived direction, a spatial predetermination or a tectonic concept. The project stems from observing and making visible what we find, refining and clarifying its readability.

For this phase, our instruments are the measured survey and the construction of large physical models of what we are observing. Without historicist criteria, we find what has value for the project. This process sometimes leads us to the unexpected, to formal and spatial solutions that surprise us and that we would never have thought, *a priori*, of drawing.

In the specific case of the Ancien Manège, once we understood its composition by parts, we conducted a study using a series of large models that explored tectonic, atmospheric and architectonic qualities of the various rooms of the building as we found them. This allowed us to understand the potential of each space for the various uses proposed by the programme.

These models and drawings were our tools for defining the strategy of intervention from a spatial and tectonic point of view. And, above all, they allowed for a more attentive study of the interventions carried out in the

1930s and 1950s, key in making us appreciate their construction quality, formal peculiarity and importance in the identity of the building.

The strategy that finally emerged was to reuse the structural elements of the nineteenth and twentieth centuries as much as possible. In this sense, we proposed precise demolitions that would clarify their reading, and that would allow the different parts of the programme to find their place within an already defined spatial and volumetric structure, adapting the brief to what the Manège provided.

New insertions were reduced to two types: stereotomic masonry, completing the existing structure and repairing the formal clarity of the building, and laminated wood partitions and floors that are reversible, give shape and adapt to the uses currently proposed.

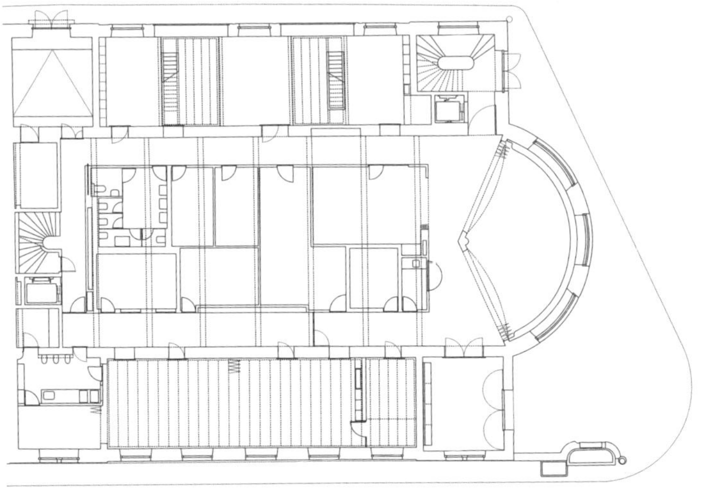

All these insertions, based on different elements that maintain their construction and material coherence, are in constant dialogue with the existing building and its context. The intention is not to establish a new formal language opposed to the existing, but rather to generate a conversation between the new elements and those already in place.

B/V.

What exists in our case is always the starting point of the project. Years ago, in a short text, "The Voice of Architecture", we wrote that our projects are always singularizations of the existing. The existing or the different realities that constitute a place—physical, atmospheric, dreamlike, intellectual—always give rise to the architectural object. In our case, what is already built is essential for starting a new project narrative. But everything is based on an interpretation, and this interpretation is inevitably the result of a cultural background that an architect gradually builds over years of training. Therefore this interpretation can only be something eminently personal. And the more personal and unexpected the reading of a reality is, the more we are fascinated by the architectures that this reading provides. The unexpected is something that we unconsciously pursue in all our projects.

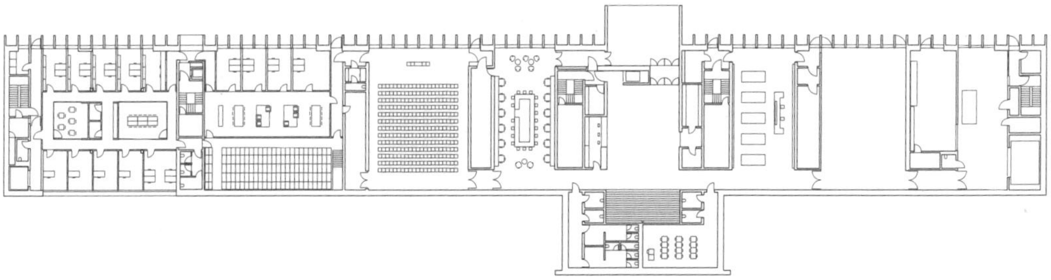

But architecture as we understand it is a discipline, and an interpretation that does not take into account its foundations will not be valid, and that is why these approaches often lose their force after a short time.

We believe that the positions that interest us most, and that we pursue, are those that are able to interpret and reuse the fundamentals of the discipline from with other perspectives, because they offer other meanings to constituent elements of architecture.

The Piece and the Entirety. Scale 3

Architectural materiality determines a key moment in the transition from an idea to a constructed reality. Currently, architects use known and new materials, and, above all, new techniques that extend the constructive and expressive (significant) possibilities of architecture.

Especially today, the increasingly technical nature of architecture requires that materiality take shape on the basis of the construction detail without losing the holistic view of the project. In this sense, there is an important debate about the relationship between the piece and the entirety.

What is the nature of the debate proposed by your project regarding materiality and technique, and consequently, the relationship between the piece and the entirety? What positioning do you think is intrinsic to your project in relation to the passage of time or a possible idea of programmed obsolescence applied to architecture?

A.

We understand the question of the piece and the entirety as in the film *Powers of Ten* by the Eamses, which establishes a kind of symmetry at the ends, between the cosmic and microscopic vision. The city is part of complexity, the economy, representation, evolution, risk and community, and we believe that a true city cannot be conceived by a single mind. And construction in the context of the Bauhaus Museum in Dessau shares this argument. Thus, for example, a true assembly of humans and non-humans has converged in the thickness of the glass, where each of these agents has inhabited the glass at its conception to jointly establish its final materiality. Time, as with the city, will change it. Complexity and change are the context, and we like Félix González Torres's expression "specific objects without specific form" to work in it.

In the German context, technique is very conditioned by processes, methodology, the industry and extensive existing regulations. The building is visibly influenced by such issues. But it also proposes a great ten-

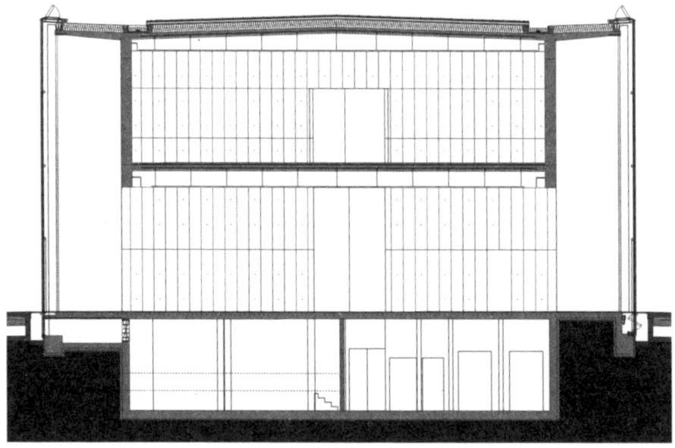

sion between them, the result of the contrast of high expectations with limited budget. It explores a very current issue, which is how to get more with less. The museum project combines the use of standard, millimetrically controllable systems (the glass façade, for example) with an interior where the bulk of the building is both structure and materiality, where the intention of using low-budget labour stands in direct contrast to German industrial precision.

We understand that there is a relationship between the whole and the parts, though there are also parts that are autonomous, such as the glass envelope (curtain wall) and the concrete bridge. Although they are different in material terms, they behave in a similar way: the glass box determines the way the building and the outer space (the park or the street) are perceived according to the properties of the material (glass: reflection, transparency), while the concrete bridge building is perceived as something heavy, both materially and metaphorically, for the content it houses.

The Bauhaus Dessau museum is a building designed to last. The concrete bridge building is structurally and programmatically independent of the glass box. So much so that the glass box has optimal proportions and modulation from the economic point of view. If the budget had been greater, the box would have been larger, but the qualities of the (almost non-existent) coatings would not have been increased. And even more evident is the relationship of the drywall interior partition with the issue of obsolescence: the partitions are fixed only to the floor and to each other, while the joint with the ceiling is reduced to a limitation against overturning, and they compartmentalize the space as if it were a temporary exhibition. In short, we trust in the BMD as an obsolescence-proof mechanism.

E.

Due to the trajectory of the studio in recent years, we have had a close relationship with architectures and landscapes of historical and heritage value, involving a rich repertoire of traditional construction solutions. These are simple solutions that arise from the properties of the materials and their capacities and limits. A tendency in contemporary construction is to try to solve each problem with a material or with a standardized solution specific to each problem. We try to explore the capacities, for example, of massive masonry walls, taking advantage of their thickness to insulate, regulate

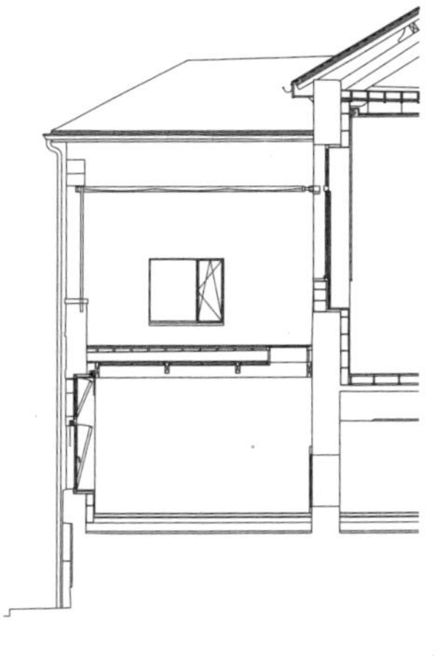

humidity and maintain stable thermal comfort, and thus avoid the transmission of sounds and improve acoustics in a single solution. The challenge in the Ancien Manège project, from a technical point of view, was to find a balance between the thermal requirements, the heritage value of the building and its surroundings, and its public use. In terms of envelope, the project proposes to increase the thickness of the existing masonry walls with another inner masonry layer with insulating capacity, allowing us to achieve the necessary comfort values while maintaining the tectonic clarity of the nineteenth-century construction. This required a lot of effort by the entire team of engineers to explore a non-standardized solution, giving rise to simple and direct constructive details.

The architectural understanding of the passage of time was a parameter included in the competition programme and an important element of our strategy. As we mentioned earlier, the new insertions are divided into two groups: first fixed structural elements, and then joinery elements that adapt to current use with the possibility of modification during the next 25 years depending on the evolution of the programme. The introduction of this tectonic dichotomy allowed us to establish an order in construction that manifests this adaptability over time.

Our project seeks to acknowledge previous interventions and add another layer in the evolution of materials and use of the building over time. We understand that our intervention in the Ancien Manège is one stage more in the history of its use and presence in the city.

B/V.

Architecture has always evolved thanks to advances related to the development of new materials, a modification or transformation of construction techniques, or the development and innovation of processes related to the discipline. It has always been like this. What has probably changed substantially in recent decades is the speed of evolution, the vertiginous change in all aspects today compared to previous times.

And this generates an extremely heterogeneous constructive landscape where each architect can explore techniques and materials almost indiscriminately. In our case, we have always been interested in giving coherence to the whole. We have always been interested in trying to ensure that a single approach to a project is able to give coherence both to the project as a whole and to its tiniest detail.

We never see our projects as aggregative elements, instead forcing their understanding as unitary, cohesive objects. That's why the idea of mass has always been part of our projects. Most of the time, we see the project as a single, modelled material. That is why we are so interested in controlling or preventing the progressive technification or hypertechnification that happens in some countries from affecting the unity of the object we build.

As regards programmed obsolescence, we never see what we do as a transitory thing, we never think of it as something ephemeral. The idea of temporary architecture, which has been part of modern thought, as we understand it, is a fraud. We are only interested in the lasting, in the enduring. And we bring this responsibility to every project we undertake.

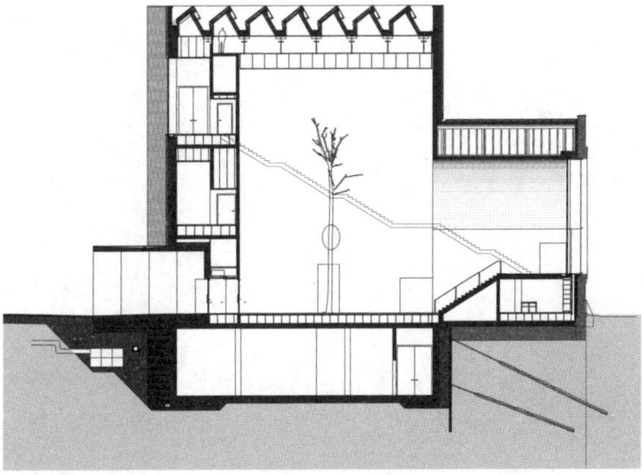

29

PROJECT: 15 Clerkenwell Close
DATES: 2017 (occupied)
ARCHITECTS: Groupwork + Amin Taha
LOCATION: London, UK
CLIENT: 15CC Limited, Amin Taha
SURFACE AREA: 2.000 m^2
PHOTOGRAPHS: Timothy Soar, except Groupwork + Amin Taha: p. 30

36

PROJECT: Chris Marker student housing and RATP bus facilities
DATES: 2007–2018
ARCHITECTS: Éric Lapierre Experience
LOCATION: Paris, France
CLIENT: RATP, Logis-Transports, SEDP, CROUS
PROJECT MANAGER: FORGUE
STRUCTURAL ENGINEER: BATISERF
MEP ENGINEER: INEX
ACOUSTIC ENGINEER: PEUTZ
SURFACE AREA: 9,655.40 m^2 (student housing), 7,170.10 m^2 (bus facilities)
PHOTOGRAPHS: Filip Dujardin, except Vincent Fillon: pp. 40–41

42

PROJECT: Fondazione Prada
DATES: 2008–2018
ARCHITECTS: OMA
LOCATION: Milan, Italy
CLIENT: Fondazione Prada
LOCAL ARCHITECT: Massimo Alvisi
EXECUTIVE ARCHITECTS: Alvisi Kirimoto & Partners, Atelier Verticale
STRUCTURAL ENGINEER: Favero & Milan, SCE Project

MEP ENGINEER: Favero & Milan, Prisma Engineering
ACOUSTIC ENGINEER: Level Acoustics
SCENOGRAPHY: Ducks Sceno
FIRE ENGINEER: GAE Engineering
SURFACE AREA: 12,300 m^2 (public), 6,600 m^2 (private)
PHOTOGRAPHS: Bas Princen, except Iwan Baan: p. 43 (bottom)

71

PROJECT: Musée Cantonal des Beaux-Arts (MCBA)
DATES: 2008–2018
ARCHITECTS: Barozzi/Veiga
LOCATION: Lausanne, Switzerland
CLIENT: DGIP (Vaud canton)
LOCAL ARCHITECT: Fruehauf Henry & Viladoms
PROJECT MANAGER: Pragma Partenaires
STRUCTURAL ENGINEER: Ingeni
MEP ENGINEER: Chammartin & Spicher, Scherler, BA Consulting
LANDSCAPE DESIGN: Husler & Associés
FAÇADE DESIGN: X-made
LIGHTING CONSULTANT: Matí AG
MUSEUM CONSULTANT: Bogner.CC
SURFACE AREA: 12,450 m^2 (gross area), 7,046 m^2 (net area)
PHOTOGRAPHS: Simon Menges

78

PROJECT: Frame
DATES: 2017 (under construction)
ARCHITECTS: Baukunst & Bruther
LOCATION: Brussels, Belgium
CLIENT: Société d'Aménagement Urbain
PROJECT MANAGER: Bureau Bouwtechniek
STRUCTURAL ENGINEER: Bollinger + Grohmann
MEP ENGINEER: Bureau d'Études Pierre Berger
LANDSCAPE DESIGN: Landinzicht (Bjorn Gielen)
TEXTILE DESIGN: Chevalier Masson
FAÇADE CONSULTANT: VS-A
ACOUSTIC ENGINEER: Kahle Acoustics
FIRE ENGINEER: Delta GC
SURFACE AREA: 9,000 m^2
RENDERING: Artefactorylab (Olivier Campagne), Maxime Delvaux

105

PROJECT:	Villa Hammer
DATES:	2014–2018
ARCHITECTS:	Herzog & de Meuron & Sauter von Moos
LOCATION:	Basel, Switzerland
CLIENT:	Private
PROJECT MANAGER:	Rapp Group
STRUCTURAL ENGINEER:	Merz Kley, Schnetzer Puskas
MEP ENGINEER:	Waldhauser + Hermann
LANDSCAPE ARCHITECTS:	Vogt
SURFACE AREA:	1,005 m^2
PHOTOGRAPHS:	Max Creasy

111

PROJECT:	Mas JEC
DATES:	2017–2018
ARCHITECTS:	Aixopluc
LOCATION:	Reus (Tarragona), Spain
CLIENT:	Private
BUILDING ENGINEER:	Pep Borràs
STRUCTURAL ENGINEER:	Ángel Obiol
MEP ENGINEER:	Josep Maria Delmuns
CONTRACTORS:	Aurea (builders of the old house), Fustes Borniquel (carpenters of the new house)
SURFACE AREA:	197 m^2 (refurbishment), 157 m^2 (extension)
PHOTOGRAPHS:	José Hevia

Quaderns #272

Editorial Board
Maria Assumpció Puig
Fernando Marzá
Francisco Rei
Josep Ferrando

Managing Editor
Francisco Rei

Directors of this issue
Nuria Casais, Ferran Grau

Articles by
Pep Avilés, David Bestué, André Bideau, Nuria Casais & Ferran Grau, Matilde Cassani, Javier García-Germán & Miquel Rodríguez, Guillermo López, Enrich Llorach, Mark Pimlott

Design
Bendita Gloria

Translations
David C. Ambler

Proofreading
Elaine Fradley

Printing and binding
Gráficas 94, Barcelona

Other photo credits:
Page 13: Wolfgang Tillmans; p. 14: Guillermo López; pp. 15–16: Pierre-Yves Brunaud; p. 18: Filippo Romano; p. 19: Jacopo Milanesi; p. 20: René Nöstler; p. 22: Courtesy of Greater Copenhagen Investments; p. 24: Georg Aerni; p. 26: Rasmus Norlander; pp. 29–35: Timothy Soar; pp. 37–38: Filip Dujardin; pp. 40–41: Vincent Fillon; pp. 42–46: Courtesy of OMA; pp. 50–69: Courtesy of the authors; pp. 73–77: Simon Menges; pp. 79–82: Olivier Campagne / Maxime Delvaux; p. 89: Courtesy of Bruther; p. 91: Didier Boy de la Tour; p. 93: Courtesy of Muoto; p. 95: Erica Overmeer; p. 97: Courtesy of Terrain-Klaus Loenhart; pp. 105–110: Max Creasy; pp. 112–116: José Hevia; pp. 119–123: Courtesy of the authors; pp. 3, 138: Adobe Stock.

ISBN: 978-84-343-1401-6
DL: B-46628-2019

Subscriptions

Artbooks
mag@artbooks.es

Bruil & Van de Staaij
info@bruil.info

Publicaciones de Arquitectura y Arte
publiarq@publiarq.com

Acknowledgments

The production of this issue of *Quaderns* has been possible thanks to the effort and the work of a large number of people. We would like to thank the Architects' Association of Catalonia-COAC and Polígrafa publishers for their vote of confidence, Rafamateo for all the initial debates, and Pep Avilés and Miquel Rodríguez for their commitment. We would also like to mention the participation of all the authors of articles and the generosity of the architecture practices and photographers who provided the documentation of the various projects published. Finally, our thanks to Bendita Gloria for the meticulous editing of the knowledge that, together, we set out to construct.

Nuria Casais & Ferran Grau

rimadesio.com

75 hna
aniversario
La Mutualitat dels Arquitectes,
ASSEGURANCES PER A TU
Coneix-nos a hna.es
PREVISIÓ
ESTALVI
SALUT
ASSEGURANCES
Tu i la teva Mutualitat
Més informació en el 933 105 522 | En la teva oficina més propera | hna.es

Lisbon ArchiTecTure Triennale

3 OCT – 2 DEC 2019

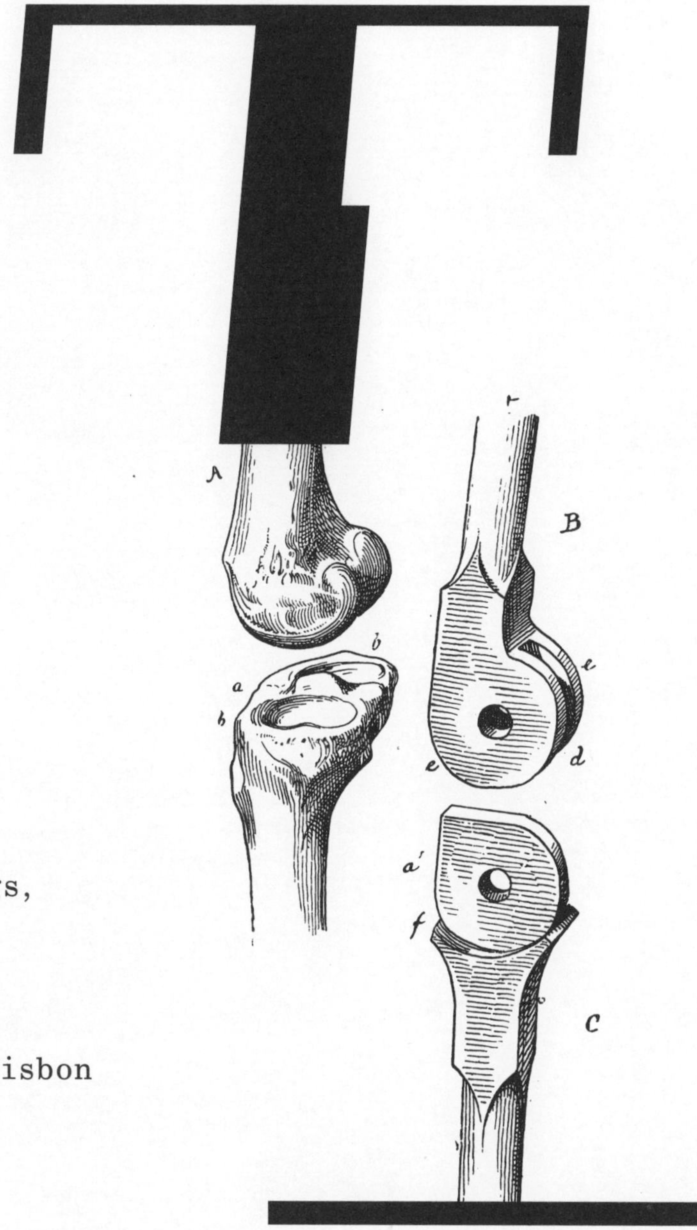

Detail of "Application des jointures des os à la mécanique" Eugène Viollet-le-Duc © Philippe Berthé/Centre des monuments nationaux | www.regards.monuments-nationaux.fr

OPENING WEEK 3 – 5 OCTOBER

ExhibiTions,
Conferences,
Seminars,
Film screenings,
Awards,
and Tours.

→ Join us in Lisbon
This fall.

Artwork: Marco Balesteros (LETRA)

The PoeTics of Reason

Strategic Partners: LISBOA Câmara Municipal; fundação edp

Program Financed by: República Portuguesa Cultura; dgARTES Direção-Geral das Artes

Member: Future Architecture Platform Member; Co-funded by the Creative Europe Programme of the European Union

Awards Patron: Fundação Millennium BCP

Co-producers: CCB; Culturgest Fundação Caixa Geral de Depósitos; Fundação Calouste Gulbenkian; maat

Institutional Partner: EGEAC

International funds: Graham Foundation

Partner: JRBOTAS

Associated Brand: ESPORÃO

High Patronage of His Excellency the President of the Portuguese Republic Professor Marcelo Rebelo de Sousa.
Competition Support: ROCK–Cultural Heritage Leading Urban Futures, Young Bird Plan. **Media Partners:** ArchDaily, Architectuul, Antena 2, Canal 180, RTP.
Support: Abreu Advogados, Cision, Dizplay. **Associates:** Babel; Casa da Arquitectura; Fundação EDP; José Mateus arquitecto; Ordem dos Arquitectos.